~ ~ ~

The Multilingual Self
An Inquiry into Language Learning

~ ~ ~

~ ~ ~

The Multilingual Self
An Inquiry into Language Learning

~ ~ ~

Natasha Lvovich
Kingsborough Community College
of the City University of New York

LEA LAWRENCE ERLBAUM ASSOCIATES, PUBLISHERS
1997   Mahwah, New Jersey

Lawrence Erlbaum Associates, Inc., Publishers
10 Industrial Avenue
Mahwah, New Jersey 07430

Library of Congress Cataloging-in-Publication Data

Lvovich, Natasha
      The multilingual self : an inquiry into language
learning / Natasha Lvovich
            p.   cm.
      Includes bibliographical references.
      ISBN 0-8058-2320-4 (pbk. : alk. paper)
      1. Language and languages—Study and teaching. I.
   Title.
P51.L88   1997
418'.007—dc21   97-6164
                                                   CIP

Books published by Lawrence Erlbaum Associates are
printed on acid-free paper, and their bindings are chosen
for strength and durability.

Printed in the United States of America
10 9 8 7 6 5 4 3 2 1

~ ~ ~

To the memory of my father who lives through this work

~ ~ ~

Contents

Foreword

Sarah Benesch

The College of Staten Island
The City University of New York

In *The Multilingual Self: An Inquiry into Language Learning*, Natasha Lvovich takes us through her experiences learning French, Italian, and English. The early stories portray her acquisition of French as an intellectual and emotional escape from difficult conditions in the Soviet Union, her native country. Next, she describes her acquisition of Italian while she and her family lived in Italy, waiting for permission to enter the United States. Later stories show that acquiring English as an immigrant forced a reckoning with everyday life in her adopted country, the United States.

Lvovich grew up in Moscow in an educated Jewish family, alienated from Soviet life. She passionately studied French language and culture to transcend the conditions of her Soviet life, to create a fantasy, to join an exclusive club. Lvovich read French literature, listened to *chansonniers*, saw French films, wrote a master's thesis on the poet Alfred de Vigny, and made French friends. Although she never imagined being allowed to visit France, Lvovich immersed herself in exported French culture and language. When, during *glasnost*, she was finally permitted to travel to Paris, Natasha felt at home in the bookstores, movie theaters, and cafés. These were the icons of the French culture she had made her own. It was only later that Lvovich began to question her attachment to French culture-for-export and to wonder if something had been missing in her relationship to French, something that might have been gained by living and working in France.

The realization that her French persona is a fantasy comes to Lvovich when she and her family emigrate to Brooklyn. Here she must confront the disheartening realities of immigrant life: searching for an apartment, for work, for dignity, for an identity. Her initial impulse is to gravitate toward the touchstones of her French life. She prowls French bookstores, eats croissants, and applies for jobs at the French consulate. It doesn't work. Her French persona is inadequate to the hundreds of tasks she must face in settling her family into their new life. Understanding this, Lvovich courageously pursues a process of self-analysis, beginning with questions about her approach to learning English and continuing with questions about her attitude toward American life and people. She senses that her use of English is superficial: "Something is missing in my way of functioning in English. Something substantial, important, that does not let me enjoy my linguistic performance. It is like I am floating on the surface of the ocean, giving curious glances into its depth." She knows, however, that to learn English deeply she must come to terms with the people and culture. Up to this point she has rejected American urban life, finding it dirty, commercial, and anti-intellectual. Now she wonders whether she can embrace it, not as a canon or set of icons, as she had done with French culture, but as a messy, frustrating, complicated, exciting mess:

> Can I love New York, love America, love people? Not the fantasy about people and about the country as I did before, but the reality? It is very hard, much harder now, because it's my reality, my life, not abstract, not literary, not poetic, and not just intellectual. While learning French, I traveled into the depth of the language because I was in love with its culture and the cream of its people, but had I ever faced the real culture, real life, real people, in all their diversity and not just mirrored in the literature and movies?

In posing these questions, Lvovich challenges herself to engage more complexly with American language and culture.

Lvovich's remarkable success in establishing a place for herself and her family in New York is revealed in the last chapters. She is a college teacher with a doctorate (on which this book is based), and has found a comfortable niche among like-minded people ("liberal intellectuals, low-income nonconformist teachers, who had difficulties confronting their own reality"). Yet, her quest for the "real" American culture, life, and people has led her to an interesting contradiction: While searching for American reality, she rejects what she finds around her, in the Russian immigrant community of Brighton Beach. Lvovich calls Brighton Beach "this isolated land in between cultures," as if it were an alien outpost, rather than an essential part of American life. She cringes when hearing the language spoken by the residents ("Ukrainian-Russian-English with a Yiddish accent"), comparing it unfavorably to her "normative" Russian. Yet as a linguist she would surely agree that all dialects are equally interesting and valid, standard written

English, African-American vernacular English, and Ukrainian-Russian-English alike.

Perhaps for an immigrant such as Lvovich, Brighton Beach is a threatening place, resembling too closely what she has always tried to escape. For second-, third-, and fourth generation Americans, such as myself, by contrast, Brighton Beach is a refuge from the superstore and mall culture that threatens to homogenize the American landscape and rob us of the remaining ties to our ethnicity. We, therefore, celebrate the Brighton Beaches and Chinatowns across the country as uniquely American neighborhoods preserving immigrant cultures.

Natasha Lvovich has the courage to pose difficult questions about how and why she learned three languages. She has written this book while still coming to terms with her own multilingualism, with how to raise her children bilingually and biculturally, and with how to understand American life. That the author has so eloquently narrated her struggles and successes in a third language will amaze language students and teachers. They will be inspired by these wonderful stories.

Preface

The Blue Man

A man wakes up one morning and with surprise sees that everything around him is blue: his bed is blue, his newspaper is blue, his wife is also blue. He leaves the house, which is of course blue, and sees that the street, the cars, the trees are blue, too. He goes to his club, drinks his blue coffee and smokes his blue cigar. Suddenly, he sees a man who is green! He says to the man, "What is going on? Why is everything blue around here, and you are green?" And the green man answers, "I come from a different joke."

The "green card" (from a different joke) says: "Resident Alien," but I am not from Mars; I am much less a geographic immigrant than a ghost from the past: after all, the Old World for many Americans, especially in New York, is related to their grandparents or great-grandparents. So I am bringing their ancestors' time and culture back to them.

Five years in America have inspired me to find my voice and to write my stories about how languages have integrated my being, defined and formed my self. The humanistic mission I am trying to accomplish—helping immigrants in their struggle with the new language—is at the same time my own struggle for a sense of belonging.

Home

For some mysterious or possibly quite rational reasons, my writing this volume coincides with my getting American citizenship. For a refugee, it means 5 years in the United States, being "stateless," and finally becoming a legal part of a community. It is an important step for me and my family, regardless of our degree of assimilation, culture shock, and English language competence. It gives me the sense of belonging, of security, of the end of immigration. From America, there is nowhere else to go; America is the end of the old historical illusion about the promised land, golden streets, escape, search for self that has nourished the Russian psyche since childhood, fed by images from Chekhov, Dostoyevsky, Gorki, and Mayakovsky. Classical Russian literature raised us in the spirit of believing that a place on earth exists where each of us could find what he or she is missing—and therefore this place was always unreachable, inaccessible, almost unreal. Russian xenophobia and later the Soviet iron curtain only enhanced that illusion. For a Jewish Russian, it was even more than that: America is the place where there was no Holocaust.

This is the end of the journey, of the odyssey of a wandering Jew, the terminal home. The language in which I am writing this book is English, and this is the first time in my multilingual and multicultural life that I can find a healthy, real voice, in a foreign language that gradually has become my own. The idea of home is certainly not connected with having a U.S. passport, or owning a house, or filling my life with familiar things—but with people dear to me, my family, my work, and my understanding of who I am. All my family—my roots and my offspring are here with me—I feel at home with my work teaching English as a Second Language, with my colleagues, with the many people I have gotten to know in America. All this creates my home. But most of all, the language of the United States, the culture, the literature is as pluralistic and multifaceted as my life as an internal immigrant back in Russia, and an external immigrant here in the United States. But is the alienating and adjusting mode of immigration familiar to any thinking individual?

I keep now the precious, yellowed-by-time, letters to the Soviet government written by my grandfather, Yakov Lvovich, from Stalin's camps, where he had to do his time as a laborer in the Siberian mines. In one of his letters, he proposed that the authorities implement a new technological invention. Moreover, he also wrote to my father, asking him to send books on mining technology. Was it mimicry? Blind faith? Self-humiliation? None of these, but rather a deep sense of respect to himself and his personal self-fulfillment. By doing the work and using his education and creativity for the government that tortured him physically and morally, and eventually killed him, he accomplished a mission superior to any political force: He did not lose himself, he did not let his spirit die.

Thus, in honor of my grandfather's dignity and all the suffering of my people, I am trying to connect the split worlds of my personality and my successful multilingualism. The price is my salvation and spiritual survival. This book is my home.

My voice in English is only one of my voices. It is the product of growth, of struggle, and of being alive; of living an ordinary life in America, where my English is a way of communication, not anymore of hiding and resisting, where my American self can become just like me. And after many years of being frustrated about differentness, I am finally at peace with it: I am like everybody else in America—different.

Finding courage—or even the nerve!—to write creatively in a foreign language, like many exiled Russian, Jewish, and other writers from different nationalities did, forced by historical circumstances, political or national persecution, is challenging. This is the choice of those who want to be heard and read, and it is also a desire to be free. Learning and using languages is a way toward freedom.

Why This Book?

The idea of writing autobiographical stories of my multilingual life has come from my long-term commitment to foreign language teaching and from my recent extremely rich and valuable experience of teaching English to immigrants in the United States. While reading and studying various aspects of second language-related theory—linguistics, psychology, anthropology and sociolinguistics literature—I realized how estranged language learners are from all that research, speculations, hypotheses, and the achievements of scholarship.

In my everyday dealings with real human souls for whom second language learning is a vital matter of survival, I have to answer questions about why their language performance is still unsatisfactory, what they should do about grammar or phonological errors, and how they can achieve fluency, overcome psychological barriers, and be themselves in a foreign language. Often, my Russian students come to my office to cry on my shoulder—so happy to be able to do it in Russian; sometimes they come to express their happiness and gratitude about their progress in English. My Haitian students share with me their writing in French (sometimes it is poetry) and are so happy to hear my Parisian accent! I love my students—maybe because all of them, regardless of their language and country of origin, are partially me: newcomers, adventurers, explorers, and learners. Once one of my ESL students asked me how long I had been in America, and commented, "I just wanted to know if it is realistic." In my stories, I try to give students like those the answer about why and at what price successful language acquisition and acculturation is realistic.

Students can learn from my stories because my tales can turn out to be their stories, too. Not only can they learn from my stories, which encourage discoveries about their own behaviors or problems, but they might want to respond, to tell us about their struggles with a foreign language. By becoming writers and interpreters of my text, by making it their own, students can construct their own virtual texts (Bruner, 1986). My stories are those of a language learner who is also a linguist and language teacher; as such they can bridge the gap between second language research and practical teaching and learning.

Moreover, this book could help initiate into knowledge language learners and their teachers. For example, a thematic college ESL or foreign language reading and writing course on second language learning could be created around this book and similar ones, calling on students to investigate and research their own language learning and familiarizing them with the most important second language theories. Experimental classes with a similar theme, with students investigating their own language learning process, have been designed and taught at the City University of New York (Withrow & Price, 1992), with very successful results. Written in a foreign language by a foreign speaker who is relatively new to the country, my book conveys this optimistic message—"You can make it!"—that every language learner needs. By reading, discussing, and writing on a topic they are personally familiar with, generating factual and linguistic knowledge through their personal connections, students will become better readers and better writers (Benesch, 1992). After all, don't they know about language learning better than their monolingual teachers do? This experience will help them to externalize the fears generated by immigration and the necessity to learn a new language; it will become in itself a "language therapy," eventually capable of lowering their "affective filter" (Krashen, 1988) that impedes language acquisition. Don't we always prefer to talk about our problems to a sympathetic and knowledgeable friend who has already gone through the experience and whose support therefore becomes more significant?

The book and the possible course that could be designed around it would create the natural "comprehensible meaningful input" (Krashen, 1988) that, according to modern research, is so important to have in a language class. My stories are written in a vocabulary and syntax accessible to advanced second language students; it is my hope that I have been able to communicate meaningfully with them. When my students read detective stories, for example, they often ask about their relevance to language learning objectives. I doubt that a question like that will arise during the reading and discussions of material directly related to language learning.

A book for second language students about their language learning and adjustment process has never been written in the United States, where a constantly increasing flux of immigrants generates enormous ESL student populations in large urban universities and schools. Living, working, and writing in Brooklyn, New York, populated at a large extent by recent immigrants, helped raise my awareness of the necessity for this type of material designed in this format. In particular, my connection to the Russian community in Brooklyn and teaching English to Russian students in college made me realize the importance of emerging from the immigrant Russian voice, from Russian historical and social context, with its characteristically distinguished cultural features.

Second language teachers and graduate students preparing for a teaching career might see this text as an illustration and a validation of the studied theory and as an inner voice of their students. They could generate questions or draw conclusions about their classroom practice and simultaneously find plausible answers in the scholarship. They could learn more about their students and become interested in some aspects of their language performance. They could disagree with some of my teaching ideas—which will engage them in thinking and prevent from a burnout. They can be creative in the interpretation and analysis of my experiences synthesizing them with their own. And this is how, amidst second language theory and teaching practice, the gap between the research and the classroom could be bridged.

Multidisciplinary by nature, my stories could be also used as a text in several college courses such as cultural anthropology, anthropolinguistics and sociolinguistics, sociology, multicultural education, ethnography, bilingualism, and the study of immigrant experience. There are numerous applications of the book in the educational field at various levels of adult learning programs that might be determined by the objectives and by the instructor's vision of it in the curriculum.

This book is also intended as a message to the general public, to all thinking individuals in search of identity: it will popularize the idea of the importance of foreign language learning, language education, linguistic literacy, and metalinguistic awareness, of illuminating self-discovery through the treasure of multilingual experience, capable of giving birth to a new, sophisticated, spiritually complex and enriched multicultural identity.

My Baby

This book looks exactly like me. While finishing the book in its initial dissertation format, I was pregnant with my second daughter, who was born 11 years after my first one. She was born a U.S. citizen from her Russian-born parents, "citizens of the world." When I saw her in the delivery room, I immediately recognized her: There was something so familiar in the way she looked that I realized I had known her all my life.

This book is the baby I was pregnant with all my professional life. The untold stories about my life in languages and cultures, my language learning and teaching experiences lay in the deep waters of my consciousness until the time came to go into labor. As with my little daughter, who was given life when my father's life was taken and many personally transformational events took place, this book also marks how my personal and professional growth evolved from a qualitative leap. The "click" that made it happen is related to the many winding roads my language teaching career took in its continuously learning mode, to supportive and interested people I met, to my study of the theory of second language acquisition, to the right time and the right place in the universe, to all the circumstances that create the right "chemistry."

The major part of this chemistry belongs to the Union Institute, which I chose for my doctoral studies, a nontraditional school full of nontraditional people, where I could grow freely intellectually and professionally, look deeply inside myself for analysis and synthesis, and integrate theory and teaching practice. I created an experiential, applied, and challenging doctoral project, based on my intensive life experience, where language would be the nexus of the complex hermeneutical relationship, subject–object–agent. My dissertation, based on my autobiography and complemented with the theoretical components, became the climax of my scholarly and personal endeavors. Language is the subject of my learning, teaching, and writing; the object of my research; and the agent, the instrument of my work and life. My dissertation made proof of the spiral movement of the language phenomena: My writing it in English, my third language, is in itself a confirmation of what my stories are about.

—*Natasha Lvovich*

Acknowledgments

I am grateful to Naomi Silverman, my editor at Lawrence Erlbaum Associates, for her knowledge gatekeeping mission: for recognizing the value of my work, for her professional involvement and response, and for her confidence in my writing. All of this has a special meaning for an immigrant and a second language writer. I am glad the world is small enough for people to meet and to recognize in each other the complex connections between generations, spirits, and values. I am honored and rewarded by this wonderful collaboration.

I thank reviewers and editors from Lawrence Erlbaum Associates for their challenging criticism, comments, and questions which generated my thinking and learning and motivated my writing. To these reviewers and editors, including Elaine Brooks, Brooklyn College, City University of New York and Vivian Zamel, University of Massachusetts, I am grateful.

Many thanks to Sarah Benesch who provoked my thinking and helped, with her professional and scholarly judgment, the vital issues of bilingualism and acculturation to emerge in my stories.

I owe special thanks to Dr. Roni Natov, my doctoral advisor at the Union Graduate School, for her intermittent support, brilliant insightfulness, and sharpness. Thanks to her, the project was born and gradually took shape. Her talented teaching of writing, careful and close guidance, her flair for art and poetry, along with her sparkling sense of humor, have created the most stimulating ambiance for my creativity. Thanks to our friendship and most intellectual sharing, I found home.

I am very much grateful to Rebecca Mlynarczyk, my doctoral committee member and colleague, for her scholarly involvement, which greatly influenced my research and teaching. I appreciated her seriousness, commitment, and dedication to teaching and her belief in the liberating power of writing, which helped me become a writer in English. I am also grateful for her participation in my work and her interest in my life.

I owe much gratitude to my other doctoral committee member, Cindy Greenberg, for bringing the updated linguistics to my doctoral project and back to my life. Along with her academic advisement, I also found warmth, friendship, and support. Together with language universals, I found the "human universals."

This book is also a recognition of the Union Institute's educational philosophy: interdisciplinarity, unconventional research methodologies, individualized approach to learning. Thanks to the Union faculty and learners, the missionaries of this philosophy, intellectual self-fulfillment and joy of learning are possible.

Special thanks to one of my peers, Susan Munaker, for the transformational role her dissertation, her thinking, and her personality played during the final revision of the book. My stories and the process of writing them has become the confirmation of her theory: "The Great Aha" is possible!

I would like to acknowledge here the significant role of the Kingsborough Community College faculty and staff; reaching out to my colleagues, I found my new world and recognized my old one. I am grateful to them for fulfilling their teaching mission, for their loyalty to and confidence in immigrant/second language students—and in me. I owe special thanks to Bob Viscount, Kingsborough ESL program director, who gave me so much of his time. Because of his fatherly push and constant professional nurturing, because of his gift of caring and for understanding of the diverse population he is working with and to his devotion to the profession, I felt included. I am also grateful to Steve Weidenborner, the English Department chairman, for encouraging me in my professional endeavors and whose genuine interest in Russian literature made me feel good about my Russian self. For all these years, I felt the sincere support of my work and of my learning of the American academic culture and language education from Bonne August, the freshman director.

My students are also part of this work: remaining in my heart forever with their individualities, they contributed to shaping my ideas and insights. It is from them and for them that this message is sent. Together we have constructed new meaning and new understanding.

I also wish to thank my family: my husband Paul, my daughter Pauline, and the baby Julia for their patience, participation, understanding, and enthusiasm. It is their sharing of me with my writing that made this work much easier; it is the whole family's sacrifice of weekends and leisure that made me work efficiently and faster; it is our unity that inspired me.

My father and my mother, too, sacrificed and invested all of themselves into my work by their understanding of my needs, their everyday encouragement, and their care for my children. Because of their investment, I was able to work with a light heart. Even though my father did not live to see the publication of this volume, he became a living part of this book. I want to thank him again. Because of my mother, I was able to finish The Multilingual Self, and with her, we have built this monument.

I am grateful to my grandparents, Mina and Yefim Novik, for joining their voices to mine by telling their life stories. Their lives are intrinsically part of me and part of this book.

I wish to thank my aunt, Ilia Novik, who is one of those most dear to me, for her interest, patient listening, and confidence in my spirit.

I also owe a special thanks to Tania and Dmitry Novik, my cousins from Leningrad/Washington, DC, for their participation, their active involvement, and their continuous support of my work, which helped me find new energy.

I am grateful to my friends in the United States who encouraged me, read, and assisted in various ways: Marc Yoffie, Tara Weiss, Paula Bernal, Jeptha Evans, Sheila Markson, Randy Thomas, Susan Roos, Tania Podrabinek, Laila Putil and Genia Yushin. Also, many thanks to my family and friends back in Russia who were interested enough to read and to respond to this representation of the new me they had not known.

—*Natasha Lvovich*

Chapter 1

My French Self

In January 1988, when I arrived at the platform of the Paris train station La Gare du Nord, I saw a small crowd of people waving their hands. They were my French friends, all of them Russian language and literature professionals, teachers, scholars, and translators who had spent many years working in Russia and who had brought real France to my apartment at Lenin Avenue. When I was getting off the train, they were all crying: My visit to France was a symbol of the opening up of Russia, of the up-lifted iron curtain, of the historic change of the world that had started with Gorbachev's perestroika, after decades of dictators' prison. Before that time, ordinary people, especially Jews, were not allowed by the Soviet government to travel abroad: Soviet citizens were all doomed to the Soviet happiness because they did not know how unhappy they really were. I always knew, however—through my friends from France, England, America, and through books—and I was unhappy. For many years I was teaching, learning, reading, translating, and writing in French—yet I could never travel to the country of my dreams to work, study, develop professionally, or see people who were dear to me. I knew from a very early age that I was being denied a number of human rights, and this knowledge grew from hatred and bitterness into a surrogate of intrinsic freedom—an aphrodisiac identity of the foreign culture and language—my France. Nobody could ever take this right from me, deprive me of this artificial world—my France—expropriate its richness and glory, repeatedly humiliate me as a person and as a professional. I constructed the walls of my fortress, and my beloved France was inside, the untouchable jewel of my creation. And because I was the center of that universe, I had to learn to do everything a French person does: speak with a Parisian accent, joke about domestic politics, sing children's songs, read and enjoy grotesque detective stories in argot as well as the most sophisticated literature, write in French in any style, curse, gesticulate, give speeches, count mentally, and dip the imagined croissant into coffee. I had to know how the French make their beds, talk on the phone, write business letters, and cook meals from different provinces. By instinct of survival, without even being aware of it, but just loving it, I made living and functioning in French my primary goal. But I never left the Soviet Union and that is the reason my friends cried when they finally saw me in Paris. The story of my fluency in French is the story of building a language identity. It was generated by my love of French culture, traditional historical ties between the two countries, but most of all by my personal way of dealing with the political regime and the sociocultural bias it created. Becoming an émigré de l'intérieur as the only spiritual and moral salvation made a foreign language belong to me: It was my Dasein, my being-in-the-world. The tragic situation of the Jewish intelligentsia in the Soviet Union, many of whom were deprived of professional careers and formal education, stimulated their learning beyond the official norms and frames, creating various unique ways for the reconstruction of self-esteem. Some became political dissidents and took enormous risks; some went insane; some turned to their religion or converted to another one. I became French.

It all started when I was 5 or 6 years old. No, before I was born, with the turn of the century generation, before and after the Bolshevik revolution in Russia, during my grandparents' generation. This is how their stories, viewed from the end of the 20th century in America, are interwoven with mine.

* * *

My grandmother, Yulia (my father's mother) together with her sister Lisa, received an excellent education before the revolution under the czar in the European-style classical gymnasium. It was a rare opportunity for the Russian Jews, who, according to the law, had to live inside the Jewish pale, now the territory of Bielarus, Ukraine, West Ukraine, and Lithuania. Without education they could make their livings as peasants, artisans, and small business owners. They were confined to little towns, called shtetls, and lived a community life well described by Shalom Aleichem and other Jewish writers. Only the most fortunate and the wealthiest, who by some miracle could make it to school in a city, would become professionals—of course only according to an official list of occupations favored by the authorities for the Jews. If needed and successful, they received the legal right to live in the big cities.

My grandmother's father was a charcoal mine engineer, an extremely respected man in his town. For his work and community reputation he was granted the governmental honor of a "legal, hereditary, and honored citizen of Russia" (with the Jewish pale stamp in his passport). These benefits and his income made it possible for him to send his children to school. Gymnasia would admit a very small number of qualified Jewish children, so my grandmother and her sister were probably well-prepared. After the equivalent of secondary school, both sisters studied in the conservatory. When the Bolshevik revolution broke out, it robbed their family, declared them bourgeois, and left them with nothing but their educational background, nobility, and good spirit. In addition to their native Russian and Yiddish, both women could speak, read, and write in French, English, and German, miraculously keeping the knowledge and skills they acquired in their gymnasium years until their death. Their knowledge, understanding, and taste for European literature, music, and art were remarkable, and their memories of everything they ever read or knew was extraordinary. I understand now that their exposure, from an early age, to intellectual and artistic discoveries, an atmosphere of learning encouraged by their parents, themselves well-educated people, must have contributed to their open-minded and liberal spirit, so difficult to retain under the Soviet terror.

I do not remember any sense of hatred or violence being expressed by or emanating from my grandmother, even though these feelings certainly would be quite legitimate due to her life situation. During the 1911 pogroms in Ukraine, Yulia's husband, my grandfather Yakov, fled to France. There he studied law at La Sorbonne, à la Faculté de Droit. After his return to communist Russia, he spent the rest of his life in Stalin's labor camps, in exile, and then in labor camps and exile again, for his "bourgeois past," for his "connections with the S–R" (Socialist–Revolutionaries party, suppressed by the Bolsheviks), for the project to bomb the Kremlin–and God knows for what else. I never knew him because he perished in the camps, but the memory of him as a noble, well-educated, honest, and hard-working man has always been present in my family and has survived in my heart. As a child, I used to dream about this grandfather who could have been everything I ever needed.

The French connection, the traditional and historical link between Russia and France since Peter the Great, could not be erased, even by the Soviet system, and was particularly important to my family, to my grandmother, to my father: It represented somehow what my grandfather Yakov had started to achieve, what my grandmother had learned and read about, and what my mother's family had dreamed about for their children and grandchildren. The noble, aristocratic spirit associated with

French culture became the unconscious aspiration of my maternal ancestors: provincial, poor, and striving for a better life. Their background is
entirely different from the other half of my family but is not less important
to reconstruct in order to understand why I became a successful language
learner and linguist.

* * *

Before the Bolshevik revolution my mother's parents lived in a small Jewish
shtetl in Bielarus and were very poor. My grandfather's mother, an early
widow, had four children and a cow with which to feed them; my grandmother's mother owned a small housewares store that was financially
ruining the family, leaving it always in debt. The children could not go to
school, except for the elementary school—the Jewish *cheder*, and had to
help their families to survive. Heartbreaking stories about my 11-year-old
grandmother's babysitting her younger sister and brother, cooking for the
family, carrying water from the river, cleaning and washing—all without
electricity, home appliances, disposable diapers, or TV dinners—picture the
isolation and despair of their reality, an impasse that was suddenly opened
into a highway by the October 1917 revolution. For them it meant liberation, possible equal rights, education, and career—all the things that had
been suppressed by centuries of Jewish segregation and apartheid in Russia.
Sleeping Jewish ambitions awoke to acclaim, lead, and participate in the
Bolshevik uprising, turning Judaism into communism, creating another God
without a human face—only for Jews to realize later that they had been
deceived, discriminated against, killed in "car accidents" and wars, and even
executed for betrayal. Most of them were convinced, faithful communists;
some of them were intelligent enough to understand that the new regime
would finally make them enter the mainstream, after centuries of social
isolation and spiritual solitude.

All over Europe, during the first three decades of the century, communism was taking hold of Jewish minds like a contagious disease, an epidemic
of liberation. My grandfather, his sisters and brothers, and many other
relatives who had been doomed to poverty were attracted by the communist
opportunities, went to colleges and became professionals, political activists
(usually one had to be a combination of both in order to succeed); some of
them took high positions in the new society, and after they and their families
were settled, they started to question what this society was about or, as they
usually put it, what it "was turning into." They did not have much time to
think, however, because Stalin's purges started and continued all the way
into the 1950s. There was also World War II, in which they defended

"Mother Russia." My grandfather Yefim ended his career as the president of one of the most important Soviet colleges, as professor of economics. He miraculously escaped Stalinist purges by leaving Moscow and retiring—"out of sight, out of mind." His brothers and sisters, cousins and relatives were not as fortunate, and many of them suffered from the regime they themselves had created. In the 1960s and 1970s when I was a child, my grandparents, with whom I shared the same Moscow apartment, along with my parents and my aunt's family, were perfectly aware of the horrors, hypocrisy, and ugliness of the Soviet system, and they never tried to hide it from me. Moreover, they rediscovered their Jewishness, as a response to growing antisemitism, and searched for their identity once lost in the ruins of communism, by celebrating Passover on May 1, the official Soviet holiday of solidarity of workers.

I remember feeling confused about being Jewish when I was in school (where I was supposed to hide it as a shameful thing) and at my grandparents' dinner table where, among stories from the Torah, there were stories about Trotsky, Mikhoels, Shalom Aleichem, Einstein, Maya Plissetskaya, and other outstanding Jews. There were stories from the clandestine Samizdat about the Holocaust, Yevtushenko's poem Babi Yar, The Diary of Anne Frank carefully hidden at the back of the bookshelf, The History of Antisemitism in Russia—the forbidden topics about the forbidden Jews; there were remembrances of the relatives lost during the war, and of course of my grandfather's liberating Auschwitz and my father's war exploits on Katyushas. I sensed and understood that there was something unique about these stories and that they were addressed to the children as a message—but a message about what? I could not decipher it and the only thing I desperately wanted was to be like everybody else—Russian—and not to know, and not to belong to the weird tribe of the killed, perished, forbidden, persecuted, tortured, executed, exiled, deprived, and caged. After all, what did it mean—Jewish? Religion? Language? Culture? I was not sure, I was torn. Did it mean to be different, to carry this differentness in the form of a stigma in the passport, of the shape of my mother's nose, of my grandparents' conversation in Yiddish, which I did not want to understand nor to reproduce? I was told at home that my Jewishness meant that I had to be the best because we are seen as the worst, that the only way to compensate for this inherited trouble was to work hard—harder than everyone else in my class or in school because my chances to succeed were minimized by my blood. As a little child I was ashamed—and who wouldn't be?—to belong to a second-rate race, and despite my family's efforts to create a good life for me, I suffered all the effects of anti-semitism in Soviet Russia, the officially proclaimed "country of ethnic harmony." The revolution swept away the orderly legal antisemitism of czarist

Russia, under which the Jewish culture, language, and traditions were segregated but legal and had a right to exist. Instead it brought about the hypocritical freedom for everybody to be the same—Russian—and Jewish culture was the first to perish. There is no people without its own culture and language, and making people feel ashamed of those things was the perfect foundation for the extermination of ethnic and cultural identity. As with any differentness, it could eventually get dangerous. And it did.

In Moscow of the 1960s and 1970s, there was one synagogue, where the rabbi was most likely a KGB colonel: How could it survive otherwise? The Jews were not admitted to colleges, especially "ideological" ones like schools for foreign languages or international relations; could never travel abroad; were not hired for "good jobs."

My confusion was growing: Could "young pioneers," "Lenin's grandchildren," be Jewish? Could I tell the secret of my Jewishness to friends? Would they reject me once they found out? Would their parents tell them to call me a "dirty Jew"? What would I do with this part of myself? Painful childhood encounters with anti-semitism grew into a resistance to consider myself Russian: I gradually accepted my differentness. Yes, my culture in the outside world was Russian culture, literature, poetry, music, ballet, and art, but I also had something else, coming from the inside. Was it my connection to the Holocaust? To Einstein and Kissinger?

Trying to figure out who I really was, I also considered my "Sovietness." But how could I be "Soviet" with my grandfather Yakov's terrifying destiny, with the truth about what was really going on in the country being revealed to me, little by little, by my parents and grandparents? Brainwashed in school and struggling for some order, I was very resistant to accept this. With time, I could not help but see with my own eyes lies everywhere around me: in every slogan in the street, in the school textbooks or on the TV screen, and injustice everywhere. My reality was definitely not the one pictured by mass media as a "happy socialist society," and the seeds of alienation and protest were planted and growing in my mind. I could not believe in, identify with, and belong to something like that; I did not know yet all the monstrosities, but I smelled something ugly—which was not mine. The Soviet ideology, with its hypocritical culture, was not intrinsically mine.

*　*　*

At 5, I already knew some French words and children's songs from my grandmother Yulia, who, surprisingly enough for her well-advanced age, was fully functional in French, even though she had not practiced it since gymnasium. It went without saying that I was to go to a school that specialized in French, where it was taught from the first grade. These specialized language schools for the gifted and talented required entry examinations: good verbal skills, basic reading and writing at the age of 6, and some general intelligence level. If I passed the test, my father promised me ice cream at the café on Gorki Street, which was very popular at that time. Even now I can remember its taste.

In addition to daily classes in French and numerous after-school French-oriented activities, the general level of education here was higher than in the average Moscow school, because the students were selected by tests and interviews. This type of school attracted a rather elite population: Soviet intelligentsia sent their children there. And some Jews did, too.

The school had strong traditions of involving children in French culture, despite all ideological restrictions, and the teachers and administration had to maneuver in the realm of the forbidden here and there in order to give us access to it. We had a famous French theater, directed by a real theater producer, with real costumes and real scenery, once even shown on Moscow television. I was in love with that theater, with my roles, rehearsals, teachers who helped with the French text, all that theater life and socialization in the ambience of French literature. Later, during junior high and high school years (in Russia, all three stages of the secondary education are called "middle school," which unifies them in one building, one administration, one philosophy), there were thematic school parties around French poetry, French songs, literary translation; there were competitions and festivals of French language and literature whose laureate I became. There were groups of French youth studying Russian, received by the school, where the students were responsible for their guests' tours, leisure, and parties. All this was possible thanks to the strength and enthusiasm of the teachers, some of whom were outstanding pedagogues, educators, and organizers. Breaking through numerous ideological regulations and restrictions, maneuvering among them was a heroic task. As many Soviet writers, who refused to adjust their creation to ideological norms, were forced to become translators to make a living—and doing so created masterpieces of literary translation—some teachers too, denied access to other, more promising careers, research, and professional or scholarly futures, found themselves in secondary schools where they could save themselves by being what they were: creative. Taking advantage of the by-product of the injustice created a positive effect for the students: We had good teachers! The system also worked in the reverse direction, placing poor professionals in higher positions. Misplacing and displacing people in the system, paying them symbolic wages, and keeping them busy with everyday problems like food shortage or lack of housing, the regime created an effect of permanent struggle for survival, of a war during peace time, and of fatalism. It was made clear to all that they were unable to control, guide, be masters of their life, that this higher responsibility belonged to higher authorities. And that this religious stance was unquestionable, indisputable, inescapable.

But this is a separate story: about these people who brought the world to me.

At home, Grandma Yulia was a recipient and simultaneously a facilitator of all my French life, information, impressions, and emotions. Because we read entire French books since the first years of studies, new vocabulary was overwhelming: Grandma used to help me with that. She also spent hours and hours with the dictionary, writing words down for me. There was a lot of memorization: dialogues, poems, whole original texts, and much retelling to do at home—so she listened and checked that, not to mention my written exercises. She used to buy French books for me (usually only classics were available) and borrowed some from her sister, who had a large French–English–German library at home and kept increasing it with the help of numerous foreign friends who were always welcome in her house.

Alive foreigners! They were considered exotic animals from Mars at the time of the iron curtain, when seeing a rare foreigner was as dangerous as reading Soljenitsin or Orwell. I felt proud to be initiated into that world, and I read, read, and read—all the things that came from real France: first children's stories, then Colette, Maupassant, Balzac, Flaubert, André Gide, François Mauriac, Hervé Bazin, Boris Vian. I went to Aunt Lisa's house (two tiny rooms in a communal apartment), smelling of paintings, book dust, and God knows how old furniture, sat on my favorite couch, with the faded green crooked seat and a shelf with a little mirror above it, attached to its back, and looked through the books, absorbing the smells and the sounds of the background—the chatting of my grandmother and her sister, a piano lesson, tea and pastry, sometimes white bread and olives, sometimes ice cream, and the ladies in multicolored robes, the neighbors. I have no memories of the "alive foreigners" but they were present in the shadows of the books and the short semi-dialogues, semi-jokes of my grandmother and her sister. Curiosity, admiration, and fascination with something that was not mine by birth but could belong to me if I really wanted it were the feelings I began to nurture at that time. The culture of Dumas and Balzac, Monet and Renoir, Edith Piaf and Yves Montand, the aristocratic intellectual world from these books and pictures started crystallizing into some kind of reality. The French reality was a French fantasy à-la-Russe, in the country where xenophobia and "xenophilia" were strangely interwoven. By using its language I could penetrate into its depth, step onto its land, and become part of it. A French personality, after all, was much less confusing and safer than being a Jew in

Soviet Russia. It was a beautiful Me, the Me that I liked: I spoke French without an accent.

I assumed my French self.

Chapter 2

Confessions of a Synesthete

A noir, E blanc, I rouge, U vert, O bleu: voyelles,
Je dirai quelque jour vos naissances latentes:
A, noir corset velu des mouches éclatantes
Qui bombinent autour des puanteurs cruelles ...

—Arthur Rimbaud, Voyelles

...- How did it begin with you?
-When my eyes opened to the alphabet. Sorry, that sounds pretentious, but
the fact is, since childhood I have been afflicted with the most intense elaborate
audition colorée ...

—Vladimir Nabokov, The Gift

I thought everybody knew what I meant when I said that in Russian six is
yellow (shest'), but my Canadian students whom I was teaching Russian to
in a "crash course" did not seem to understand. They looked at each other,
perplexed: what a crazy teacher they had! She did not know how to drive,
she spent her life reading, and she firmly stated that six was yellow. I guess
they referred that one more oddness to the general "exoticism" I represented
for them and never took this weird idea seriously. Only much later I realized
that my color associations did not necessarily coincide with other people's,
and that for the most part people don't think in colored words at all, like I
do. Once, driving among canola fields all covered with bright yellow flowers
with one of my Canadian cowboys, I heard him saying, "Look, Russian six
is growing!" I was happy then that my "exoticism" helped him to memorize
the word, and some shadow of thinking about my strange faculty and the
possibilities of using it in foreign language teaching started to form in my

11

mind. That is when I found, reading Nabokov's memoirs, the word *synes-thesia* instead of *exoticism*.

Thinking about synesthesia now makes me wonder why I never tried to investigate my strange faculty since I had always been aware of it. Perhaps I had honestly believed some of it, like numbers and days of the week, was part of every human experience and served, among other mnemonic strategies, as a memorization technique (it turned out I was not exactly wrong there). On the other hand, I had probably sensed that people's startled looks and uncertain smiles in response to my story mirrored the reaction to something definitely wrong, similar to a mental disorder—and I had repressed my questions and further self-analysis. During my childhood and school years, being Jewish was enough of a "disability" for some other disability to be questioned. In college, I became more accepting of my own mental extravagances and started questioning the strange mechanisms happening in my bilingual head. It was probably much later, when I became fluent and fully functional in English, that the question of words and colors re-emerged. Perhaps, the linguistic and metalinguistic experience got accumulated and condensed into awareness, or immigration forced me to look closely at myself and find emotional peace with my languages and cultures. As a result, I began inspecting and labeling the colored sensations in my multilingual storage.

In English, six is whitish, fuzzy, dull glass; in French, creamy in color and substance. In French, *Lundi* is pale wax pink; in Russian, *Ponedel'nik* is grayish and dull; and Monday is in orange–red–brown gamma. I could give this type of characteristic to every word, sound, syllable, expression in every language I know, giving myself time to think, feel, and sense it. In some cases it would be easier to associate sounds, with an object shape, smell, or touch. Or just say: It is like this apple, or this music, or this experience. That is why the game of "The Chinese portrait," which asks you to think about a person in terms of the weather, music, architecture, cars, or furniture, has always made perfect sense to me. I play it with my students for linguistic purposes in any language I teach, and they usually enjoy it because they discover that their world of abstract, intellectual, and sensory associations is much richer than they tend to think. Are these mental activities connected to language processing? If so, can we develop them the way I did in order to trigger second language acquisition mechanisms?

The very act of writing this makes me feel as if I am physically dragging objects in space from one place/dimension to another, like you would move a heavy sofa—and then look at it from a different angle, attempting to see its newness in the whole picture of the room. It feels as if the things I am trying to describe here just belong to a certain "place" in my mind, are part of my mental functioning, and do not "want" to be displaced in the area of verbalization. After all, does it feel right to describe the process of walking?

When I began learning English in college, I had a hard time memorizing the days of the week. They seemed colorless and all similar until the day when I started consciously thinking about their colors, and they finally appeared bright and all differentiated. It was like the black-and-white movie suddenly turning multicolored, gaining a system of meaning with it. Monday got orange–red; Tuesday—almost black, dark navy; Wednesday—watery silver; Thursday—grayish airy transparent; and Friday—dark purple. The more I thought about that, the more nuances of colors, shapes, even perceptible flavors I could define. The fact of living with "colored hearing" or "heard vision," the combination of sound–letter–color happening in my mind added an extraordinary, sensory dimension to everything I was doing mentally and creatively.

My attempt to explain this complicated sensation is close enough to the metaphor of a dream description; how many times have we experienced the impossibility of describing in exact terms what our dream was about! Its content, surrounded by sensations and images, simply does not entirely fit a human language or vice versa: The map does not cover the territory! The exercise leaves us unsatisfied and frustrated with our vain attempts to rely on words. This is how I feel, verbalizing my synesthetic experiences.

In my sleeping existence, as well as in my waking one, my dreams reflect my colored linguistic reality: I often see in my dreams a word or a syllable that has no meaning: it is pure form, in its colored stereo-optic suspension in space, often funny or scary or smelly; it is sometimes a complicated multicolored verbal expression with a stinging sharp suffix that makes me cough and generates a puff of various interrelated physical and mental sensations; it might be a person pronouncing a sentence that I perceive visually and aurally in the luminous splash of shapes, colors, light—which creates a meaning beyond the sentence and makes the ordinary semantic meaning fuller, richer, and more complicated in a verbally unexplainable way. Is there a language beyond human languages whose elements become visible to a linguistically trained mind while the consciousness is asleep? Or is this just an expression of an emotional reaction to "life in languages"?

The colored images accompanying my learning, and in particular language learning, must have facilitated the language acquisition, "sensorily" providing extra support to this creative process. Memory, among other mental activities, is the obviously affected area since the synesthetic ability could be used as a mnemonic device. I figured that out long ago, long before I learned the word *synesthesia*. This capacity to recall words thinking of their colors or imagining them pending in the air, while examining their shape, smoothness, position in space, or feel at touch I termed "good visual memory." I knew I would never forget the word once it was imprinted in my mind in clear sensations by reinforcing other mnemonic techniques like the context, associations, or emotional background. In order to do that, I always have to see the graphic sign, either on paper, or in my mind—spelled. When English became my "first," functional language in the United States, I noticed how obsessed I became with spelling. Of course much of my good spelling skills comes from my linguistic background, knowledge of French, and the well-trained ability to generalize about language rules, but a lot of it is due to the synesthetic memory that helped me to remember the sound–letter combinations with extra sensory support. For example, I recently learned the word *resilient*: a brownie, with a cutting silver edge. Its sensory image will "call for" the word. The semantic meaning, like in my dreams, seems to be living its own life and is not really connected to the image of the word form.

My visual memory will never fail me in the geography of an unfamiliar city, with telephone numbers or names if the visual means supply enough "sensory meaning," colors, particular shapes, or smells that could be transformed into a mnemonic technique. (It is easy to understand why highlighting, marking, and note-taking become so significant and how important the colors and the quality of pens, markers, and pencils become!)

I attribute the sensation of *déjà-vu* to the same type of nebulous phenomena as my synesthesia. It is sometimes a *déjà-entendu* or *déjà-vécu*, when I know that the visual, auditory, or all together experienced event happens for the first time in my life—yet in the back of my mind I have already lived, heard, and seen it. Putting aside the metaphysical, one plausible interpretation is the synesthetic one: the association of sensory impressions of some past experience—the colored, shaped, and heard—echoes to a new sensation somewhere at the intersection of the "normal" brain processors and the "sensorily blended" ones.

* * *

Depending on the phonetic features in each particular language I know, the letter-sound has in my mind its own color–shape representation: If the sound is very similar, like "s" in French, English, Russian, and Italian, it differs in shade or in stereo-optic dimension in my mental space, which could be tentatively called a "positive linguistic–sensory transference." Its representation varies with the combination of one sound–letter with another sound–letter, producing its own image. The word could be represented by the dominant color of the first letter-sound or by the combination of the images of its syllables, bringing about a multicolored picture, very often associated with a tactile sensation. My daughter's name, Pauline, for instance, is a combination of gray and pink and resembles in French the feel and looks of the little stuffed mouse that she had been carrying with her from Moscow to Europe and to America. This Jewish mouse, by the way, had traveled from France to Russia, and then emigrated with us, like in the popular Disney cartoon *The American Tail*. Pronounced in English, however, the sensation of the name changes into something colder, almost icy, and the pink is whitish and hard, not at all like the stuffed Jewish mouse.

With different sounds or combinations of sounds varying across languages, there appears the whole sensory picture and gamma of colors for each particular language, which might be one reason for the difficulty I have always experienced switching from one language to another ("negative linguistic–sensory transference"). The switch feels almost mystical like entering a different world, stepping onto an alien territory, adjusting the layers, or visualizing a rainbow. With my increasing attempts to observe, describe, and classify this "head stuff," it increasingly appeared more metaphysical, parapsychological, and poetic. But when I started researching it, inward and outward, more physical, psychological, and linguistic facets started to emerge. The traits that I have discovered made me look back at the stained glass of my childhood, where my life in colors and languages had started.

* * *

The Bolshoi, with its soft wine-colored velvet seats, golden ornaments and fringed curtain balconies, was the immovable feast of my childhood, the symbol of the authentic mythical Russia, the happy Christian reality of Pushkin, Tolstoi, and Pasternack accompanied by music from Chaikovsky's fairy tales. *The Nutcracker, Sleeping Beauty, Swan Lake*, in their strictly classical versions, with the world famous ballerina Maya Plissetskaya, a boneless angel and a fleshed demon, were a celebration of eternity. Along with the best of Russian culture, the classical ballet survived the worst times of Soviet decay and stagnation. The Bolshoi never oppressed me with its palatial grandiose beauty; instead it enchanted my ordinary life and poured magic into it, so that colorful stories continued their life in my mind after their life on stage. Performances, concerts, New Year's costume parties were all transformed into colorful albums: "books" of fairy tales, with the text on one side of the album, and the picture on the other. Later on, my fascination with folk and theater costumes began, enhanced by adventure books and historical novels. These books rarely had any pictures or contained only the black-and-white sketches that seemed unattractive to me; so I made my own, recreating the books or inventing my own stories. Then science fiction, and then stories of American Indians followed, in crayons and watercolors—multicolored plumages, brown faces, aquiline noses. They were as fictitious to me as the princes and princesses of the fairy tales. I drew them only from imagination, attributing forms and colors to what existed only in my mind. Television and movies were almost nonexistent for Russian children, so the visual information from the screen did not affect me. I was always very bad at still lifes, landscapes, and portraits that I perceived as copying. If the colors and shapes had already formed an image in life, I did not see why I had to create my own. Drawing and painting—my favorite pastime—allowed my imagination to find its visual pictures in the interchangeable worlds of reality and fantasy.

In the elementary school, where French was taught beginning in the first grade, much emphasis was placed on visual aids. There were pictures for words, pictures for letters, pictures for linguistic games, and a paper puppet theater that we created and with which we acted out plays. We also had to draw a picture, representing every French "vocabulary word," for spelling.

Once there was the word *crow* and I could not draw it! I saw it so clearly, however, like hearing a melody in your mind without being able to reproduce it. Grandmother Yulia took me to her sister, Lisa, who lived in the old Moscow bulgakovian house in a communal apartment, where along the dark, scary corridor there were perhaps more than 15 rooms, each inhabited by women in old-fashioned black-and-yellow silk robes with complicated pre-revolution names like Azalia Emilievna or Yevripida Grigorievna. They seemed to live in a different dimension of the world, and I was curious and frightened to smell their last century rooms or to meet them in the corridor where they walked back and forth to the kitchen, with their tea kettles.

At my Aunt Lisa's, I met her son and his wife, both artists. They drew a crow in my vocabulary notebook. This crow of my childhood has become an autograph of the future artistic director of the Bolshoi, Valery Levental. His wife Marina also worked for the theaters and created wonderful cartoons for children. That house and that part of my family from my father's side appeared as an oil-painted background of the theater stage of my childhood. Its action was taking place at the avant-scene, but the scenery complemented the performance by the smell of old books and oil paintings hung all over the place and by Aunt Lisa's piano music strangely associated with the colors and the smells of the paintings. Interestingly enough, I cannot recall any conversations or words, any attitudes displayed to me or in front of me, as if this house was completely deprived of contents. It seems that I witnessed its life on a silent screen, incorporating its vivid artistic form into a sensory, nonverbal lot, nested in the back of my mind.

My serious artistic inclinations were interrupted by an unfortunate incident. When I was about 10, my grandfather from the mother's side decided that I had a gift worth attention and put himself in charge of its further development. He was determined to expose my "talents" to an educational enterprise, demonstrating traditional Jewish intentions to value education and transmit this value to children and grandchildren. He took me to a painting class in the Palace of Pioneers, some old Russian prince's residence transformed into a children's activities place, with the slogan, "Art belongs to all the people. V. I. Lenin," at the front door.

The lessons were boring: we had to draw in pencil Greek vases or Venus' arm or leg, or a still life, an apple on a plate—I resented that. The teacher was probably boring, too: at least he did not pay any attention to my perception of copying as absurdity. I was not willing to learn the technical rules of drawing or painting; I was more interested in expressing on paper the colorfully shaped images from my imagination.

Sometimes I think that my resistance to that violence against my artistic potential, along with my desperate desire to break the tight family chains, was so strong that it engendered the following incident that put an end to my educational torture. Once, when my grandfather left me at the "palace," intending to pick me up after class, I discovered that the class was cancelled and the "palace" was empty. I was alone and walking around the endless hallways and lobbies when a man suddenly stopped me and started touching me and doing something to me that I could not understand. I managed to free myself and run away, and the only things I remember of this horrible run are locking myself in the bathroom; a girl who told my grandfather where I was hiding; the presence of a woman, the director or the administrator of the "palace"; and the police. The rest of it is completely blank, except for the vague recollection of the big family reunion in the kitchen, of the Yiddish words, the words in Russian that sounded as incomprehensible as Yiddish, and of my trying to understand what a "sexual maniac" was. Since that time I never again went anywhere else to learn how to draw. Instead, my grandfather took me for choreography/artistic skating lessons. I never liked that, but according to my grandparents, "children had to be developed."

Art accompanied my childhood at the Moscow Tretyakov Gallery of Russian Art, the Pushkin Museum of Fine Arts, and numerous art exhibitions—there were always important cultural events, that were impossible to miss. Art was present everywhere I traveled with my parents: the Hermitage and the Russian Museum in Leningrad and small art collections in Estonia, Latvia, and Lithuania, not to mention the golden, bright, simple colors of the Orthodox churches and pale and grayish Catholic cathedrals. The books that filled my life with beauty continued to evoke imagery and colored expression—and I drew my favorite musketeers, Le Petit Prince, and Anna Karenina. Later, something else continued the visual dimension: it was poetry. My early familiarization with Russian and French poetry, writing and translating poetry, using both languages since my early teen years, the yet imperfect attempts to fit my synesthetic images into the literary, verbal performance became a mode of seeing and gaining freedom of imagistic expression.

* * *

The confessions of a synesthete sound "tedious and pretentious," in Nabokov's (1966) terminology poignantly reflecting the essence of this attempt that appears snobbish and elitist to describe the undescribable. Hopefully, they will add a drop to the ocean of knowledge about self as an impressionistic self-portrait.

On a humorous literary note suspended in my multicolored and multidimensional universe in the form of a delicious sundae for dessert, is the "synesthetic novel" dear to my heart and my senses, Mood Indigo, by the remarkable French writer, poet, and jazz musician Boris Vian (1968). Like "Nabokovese," Vian's language and intratextual organization is abundant in synesthetic metaphors. Here is one of them, picturing the main character's invention, "pianocktail," which produces beverages out of the melodies played. For example, Duke Ellington's Blues of the Vagabond makes a cocktail "all the colors of the rainbow" that "tastes exactly like the blues," (p. 137) and Misty Morning "produces a cocktail that's pearl gray and mint green, and tastes of pepper and smoke" (1968, p.137).

> Each note corresponds to a spirit, a liqueur, or an aromatic.... The loud pedal corresponds to beaten eggs and the soft pedal to ice. For soda you need a trill in the upper register.... There is only one thing which is annoying, and that's the loud pedal for the eggs. I've had to put in a special system of interlocking gears because when you play a tune that's too hot, bits of omelette fall into the drink and it's hard to swallow. (pp. 13–14)

Chapter 3

"Magister of the Game"

Magister dixit.

—Latin proverb

He came from the 19th century. Half Rastignac, half André Chenier. In the fall, He wore a deep-green felt hat, of the same color as the water at *Chistiye Prudy* (Clear Ponds), where He lived, the old Moscow neighborhood with two- or three-story houses, former residences of Russian upper middle-class aristocracy. He used to carry to class a clean piece of cloth in a tiny plastic bag: after using the blackboard, He carefully wiped His hands and put the cloth back in its bag, with an expression of extreme dissatisfaction and disgust, as if this simple action reflected the paradox of His life.

He was as distant as a stranger, as handsome and noble as a prince, as unearthly as a fallen angel. He did not seem to belong to the reality He lived in, to Moscow of the 1970s, except for its caricaturish shadow—the bulgakovian Moscow, the blend of gospel, mysticism, and the post-NEP[1] kitschy fantasy of the 1930s. He was a strange representation of the Soviet paradoxical picture of paganism and Orthodox Christianity, of Stravinsky, and of tramway bells instead of church bells. The favorite character of the European 19th century literature, a *déraciné*, out of his time and society, He was very lonely and unhappy. The image He was creating of Himself out of His favorite literary masterpieces did not have to be His real self: After all, how did that matter to those who were able to touch the beauty of His spirit?

Teaching young teenagers was not the great cause of His life, but thanks to some higher will, it was the mission He assumed. His misfortunes offered me and, I am sure, other students of His great causes and discoveries He

---

[1] New Economic Policy (NEP) is the economy of "temporary capitalism" that allowed for limited private enterprise, introduced by Lenin in the 1920s.

might have missed. He was one of those who brought the world to me.

I know very little of His life story. Allegedly He had worked for communist big shots, translated for Khrushev, suffered from party nomenclature purges, was fired with no future opportunities for a career, chased away from the top. Supposedly He descended from an old Russian aristocratic family; He lived with his aunt, after his mother's death, in a communal apartment with dusty windows overlooking Chistiye Prudy, the tramway bells ringing all day and all night. All I remember is dusty, foggy, thick air, the smell of oil from the icons and paintings, crystal port glasses, last century furniture, and the dying pale, violet flowers on the gray marble windowsill.

I was 14. When He walked into the class and said, "Bonjour," I cried out, very loudly, "Ah!" I was initiated. It was like opening a book, looking at the first page—and discovering literature. It was like recognizing the exact meaning of words, after having seen them repeatedly. But most importantly, it was seeing the future. When I saw Him and heard Him pronounce the first sound, I wanted to become who I have become—as a person, a scholar, a professional, and a woman.

I was one of the few students He communicated with in school. His teaching style was as elitist as His taste. He believed that those who want to learn will hear His message; those who do not want to learn do not deserve any attention; those who are unable to learn will live in misery. He often publicly shamed and humiliated students who were lazy or intellectually limited and was notoriously hated—as passionately as he was adored. He taught French and French Literature; He also led an optional extracurricular weekly session on the linguistics of French media.

I was in His class for about 2 years. I was following Him in the exciting linguistic adventures in French polysemy, synonymy, antonymy, etymology, phonology, and phraseology. Learning the language with Him was learning about the language along with using it. Both parts of the process were interconnected and systematic: I enjoyed the logic of His teaching, His philosophy of the need to apply theory to practice, which could be clearly observed in the way He taught French literature. The issues in the texts we read and discussed referred not only to "what," but "how" and under what historical circumstances. Not to mention that the classes were led exclusively in French, no matter what the linguistic difficulty of the topic or its analysis.

The factual material of His class was challenging and reached beyond the frames set by the Soviet ideology: we were passionately initiated in the best of French writers and poets whose work was inaccessible to the average reader. Our intellectual journey included the profound analysis of the French symbolist poets, the challenge of the surrealists, and the depth of the classical literary heritage of Hugo, De Vigny, Musset, Balzac, Maupassant, Flaubert. At His media workshop, I learned to read between the lines of the only available French newspaper in the Soviet Union, *L' Humanité*, trying to taste with my tongue various language styles. He used to point out an idiom, a metaphor, or an expression—and savor it in His mind, with His voice, in His mouth—as people do with delicious refined food, pulling it from one cheek to another and clicking with His tongue. In French and in Russian, "tongue" and "language" are the same word: With him I learned how to physically taste words. That was the time of my first attempts to write poetry in French and translate from French into Russian. Creativity is generated by strong emotional impulses—especially at 15. Was I in love with Him? The idea had never occurred to me. He was above humanity and therefore beyond my reach. I only wanted then to get access to his club. I am a member now.

After I finished school and was getting ready for college entry examinations, working day and night on French theoretical grammar, Communist Party history, Russian composition and literature, I told my parents, who were doing the impossible to get me in, that despite all that load of studies, I needed a couple of hours a week of French conversation, and that I wished He could do it. I guess I just needed the presence of His spirit in my intellectual efforts, the warmth of the real language, the taste of the words, the ambience of culture and literature. The life of the Soviet intelligentsia at that time was at the edge of poverty. School teachers could hardly survive. My parents offered Him generous pay for His tutoring. He refused the pay but offered to see me once a week. I am sure it was not an act of charity but the ability to see into the future. Did He know about the story I am writing now?

We used to sit on a park bench, next to the pond, watch black swans, and speak French. Sometimes I had to solve the most exciting linguistic puzzles out of various derivatives, dealing with the history of French, with Latin roots, geography, and ethnography. Later, in college, I found out that what we were doing was part of the field of historical linguistics, a course I was extremely interested in. We also played with the idioms by semantic topics such as clothes or food or weather. We amused ourselves with all kinds of verbal games and sometimes He brought me something interesting to read. But for the most part, He was my book, my newspaper, my cinema. I enjoyed that interaction—and I was learning.

It was an unusual student–teacher environment, under the trees of an old Moscow summer park, where kids were playing and yelling, grandmothers with their knitting were chatting, and old men were playing chess. When it rained, He took me to an ice cream café where my main preoccupation was to keep my French dignity in the humiliating atmosphere of Soviet public service. I remember clearly how conflicting all these "outside" inconveniences were with the vision of the "inside" world that He transferred to me and that we now do share.

To "exist" means to "stand out" in Latin (*ex-sistere*). He existed, he stood out for me. Like a stereoscopic picture, He represented what stood out and what I was searching for: brilliance, originality, spirit—as hope, direction, and connection to meaningfulness. The world in which we lived in the Soviet Union of the 1970s was a *kitsch*, a cheap print, a caricature, and its tragic narrative in the absurd, represented by people like Him, was a message to the future, to me. I got the message.

Living and writing my stories in the United States of the 1990s, in the New World, where European history is gradually disappearing and something new, and so old, is being born, I am wondering about that Old World man or my fantasy of that man, who taught me the concepts of the above, between, and beyond. These concepts are most significant in my postmodernist new world.

The glory of His erudition connected history, literature, poetry, music, and other humanities into a whole: It was an ingenious game with its own sophisticated rules and systematicity, where everything acquired a multifaceted, spiritual, almost cosmic meaning. About 10 years later, I read Herman Hesse's *Game of Beads* and recognized there my Castilia, my educational efforts, and my "Magister of the Game."

That key to existence, to "standing out" that He gave me has been always with me, in my linguistic, professional, scholarly, and intellectual encounters. My favorite occupation—learning, teaching, and living languages—is to embrace and give out the new experience.

I recognize His presence when I walk into my English class and talk about American literature as my own. When I see my students' eyes, looking inward but also very passionately at me, I know they are with me on the journey. I hear then my 14-year-old "Ah!" as an echo of time.

Chapter 4

Messengers and Mediators

C'étaient pas des amis de lux'
Des petits Castor et Pollux
Des gens de Sodom' et Gomorrh'
  Sodom et Gomorrh'
C'étaient pas des amis choisis
Par Montaigne et La Boétie
Sur le ventre ils se tapaient fort
  Les copains d'abord.

—Georges Brassens, *Les Copains D'abord*

Domka

Saturday mornings were not much different from other mornings because my 2-year-old daughter, like all kids of her age, used to wake up early. She woke up, full of energy and happiness, and propelled herself from our bedroom to the living room, and then to the kitchen. I would not have been as happy as she was if I had not seen the little white sneakers at the front door. I am still wondering how they could possibly be so clean and so white, with the dirt, water, and mud all over Moscow streets, at all seasons, either from rain or from snow. The tradition of having guests take off their shoes at the entrance of the house and owning a stock of home slippers to offer them must have come from the historical "muddy Russian roads" rooted in the continental climate conditions. The white sneakers looked like she had flown to Lenin Avenue from the train station. They were so much like her: neat, cream-polished, with washed laces, and tiny—kid's size.

Hurray! Domka was there! I sniffed the air: the smell of Camels (ka-mel, pronounced in French) was coming from the kitchen. She was sitting at the

23

table, so much at home, with her coffee and buttered black bread. She is short and boyish: a miniature of a French liberated woman. I knew then: my day would be enlightened.

Dominique (Russian nickname Domka) taught in the Soviet Union on contract with the French government. Her first-year assignment was teaching French at the university of Smolensk, the little town on the outskirts of Central Russia, and of course she was overwhelmed with the experience of the Russian province. Almost every weekend she took a Friday night train and arrived in Moscow early on Saturday morning. She had her own key toour apartment and she quietly snuck in, made herself coffee, read, and waited until we awoke.

I had known her for so many years that she felt at home everywhere my family was: at my parents', my aunt's, and my father-in-law's where we lived. When I met her, translating for a group of French lycée students in the mid-1970s in Moscow, sinking in the ridicule of Brezhnev's speeches and everlasting comic drama of the communist authoritarian regime, I discovered the spirit of François Villon and May 1968 in Paris and the liberating and liberal voices of Georges Brassens, Georges Moustaki, and Renaud. She had chosen Russian as her major at the Paris Institute of Eastern Languages and visited Moscow and Leningrad as often as she could: often twice a year. When she held her master's in Russian studies, she applied for a teaching job in Russia; she had also started her doctorate, specializing in the work of Isaac Babel. Her interests in Russian culture and language and mine in French created the perfect intellectual coalition; her friendship, generosity, and authentic care offered across the border made us, oppositely different personalities, close friends. This friendship, worshipped over more then 15 years, was the best gift I ever received. It was a holiday friendship, a celebration of the real, not the Soviet hypocritical spirit of internationalism, where our souls and cultures blended and dissolved, and where enjoyable reciprocal learning was taking place.

It was also an example of interfamily relationships across the border: Our mothers, the one in France and the one in Russia, took care of Domka and me as their own daughters. Dominique was not only our liaison with the outside world, but a rescuer; she regularly supplied us with medicine for my sick father (even aspirin was not available then in Russia), with books and tapes for me, as necessary for my survival as medicine for my father, with clothes and baby items for my daughter. She took the risk of assisting my family of refusniks, the outlaws who had been denied the exit visa for 10 years, to keep in touch with the rest of the world, because our international and domestic correspondence was strictly censored. She was our ears and our voices. She was also a joy. We all loved her as the family child. It was the Russian–French symbiosis, the incredible closeness of cultures and people, separated by the physical, moral, and informational wall of the iron curtain.

Once, on a beautiful sunny day in May, she called me from Smolensk; her voice sounded very alarmed from her first "Salut!" She had just gotten a telegram from the French Embassy, ordering all French employees to evacuate the area: Smolensk is located at the border with Bielarus—Chernobyl is not far away. That is how I found out the horrifying news. The Soviet government did not make any announcement; nor did it order evacuation. Instead, it let thousands of people, with their children, march in the deadly contaminated air in the streets of Kiev, Gomel, Smolensk, and other neighboring cities to celebrate the triumph of the Soviet nation on the Day of Solidarity of Workers. I called Paris; they knew already. Domka's mother was worried to death. I told her Domka was coming to Moscow and would get a medical check-up by French doctors. Russia still did not know.

When she arrived, our apartment was transformed into a Chinese laundry. My husband, Domka, and I boiled, steamed, washed, and ironed all her clothes and belongings. We also decided to call up everybody we knew to inform them about the accident and advise them about taking precautions with food. Many were getting ready to receive their friends and family from Ukraine and Bielarus.

Domka never returned to teach in Smolensk. However she went there years later, to meet people she had known and with whom she had become friends.

We shared happy moments, too. Parties, holidays, trips, common friends. Domka played the guitar, we sang French songs. We seemed to be born with these songs, in Moscow and Paris alike. I often remembered the lyrics that she tended to forget. We used to have those laughter attacks from eye contact that only close people, with a common philosophy of life have: only we two knew the reasons for these explosions of hysteria, and my parents always said, "Look at these two. They always get this when they get together!"

Domka was famous for not eating; she seemed to survive on coffee and cigarettes. I found out later from her mother, who feared anorexia, that only my mother's cooking and my own cooking had made a difference; she could not resist my mother's pirozhki and cakes, and she loved long Russian dinners, with people sitting all evening long, eating, drinking, talking, and singing.

The language she and I spoke was French. It was also the language of our correspondence, of all our friendship and sharing, of common interests, of humor, of our relation to the world. With Domka, I forgot which language I spoke, heard, and functioned in. It was our language.

It is easy: If people want to understand and be understood and to love and be loved, they have to speak the same language.

Marc and Julia

Marc and Julia were a funny couple. They claimed they had to get married in order to be able come to the Soviet Union to work. If they were unmarried they would not have been able to live in the same hotel room in Moscow and would have gotten themselves in all kinds of trouble; cohabitation was considered a sin in conservative Soviet Russia.

Julia studied with Domka at the Institute of Eastern Languages at La Sorbonne; Marc was their teacher. He had spent all his life studying Russian language and literature and was famous for his erudition. He seemed to know everything about everything: a real "walking encyclopedia"! But not only that: he used all that knowledge with a refined and humorous charm in the most mundane situations and created meanings of everything around him. He spoke Russian with a slight Baltic accent, interspersing his speech with literary quotations from various Russian classics and swear words, used most creatively. Julia, 25 years younger, appeared to be his mother because he exhibited such an inability to deal with practical matters and everyday situations that she had to take over the role. But aren't geniuses always forgiven? I always suspected the distribution of roles did not entirely reflect the reality about what Marc really could and could not do; he was an intelligent bon vivant who knew how to assume his role best.

Julia and Marc had many friends all over Russia; most of them were poets, musicians, or bards forbidden by the regime. Some of them were just miserable intellectuals. They often told me I was different from the rest of their Russian friends because I did not seem so miserable. All the Russians were doomed to the role of "poor nephews" in their relationships with foreigners, because any foreigner seemed to be a millionaire in Russia, not to mention the privilege of traveling, using information, and many other ingredients of the life of a free human being. Relationships with people then became preconceived and a priori unbalanced; I was happy ours was more or less equal. Not as a communist but as an idealist I believed in real equality based on intellectual, not material possessions.

Marc loved Russia. He liked to repeat that Russian experience had a nostalgic touch for him: it reminded him, in its economics and spirit, of his childhood—France under Nazi occupation. This multifaceted historical connotation was half joke, half reality, like everything Marc's wit produced.

Thanks to the interactions with our foreign friends, we learned a lot about our country and ourselves, because only the view from the outside and about the outside reveals much about the inside. I realized at that time that learning foreign languages with their cultures helped me to be more self-reflective and analyze things that had been considered as given and unquestionable; contrast and compare, be systematic, find parallels and cyclic movements in the history, civilization development, and the nature of human being. In other words, contact with languages and cultures stimulates cognitive, mental, and intellectual growth.

Marc and Julia provided their Russian friends with food from the hard currency store and often with money; they took their friends' manuscripts to France and submitted them for publication; they organized in Paris all kinds of popularization and awareness-raising activities to inform French intellectuals of the political situation in Russia, of the existing subculture, of the sleeping or put to sleep Russian geniuses. They knew the group of active Russian émigrés, exiled to the west, and put themselves at risk, helping them and their families, left behind.

The world knows very little about the role of these messengers from the west in Soviet society during the last three decades of its existence. Their spiritual input in dying Soviet Russian culture and the profound respect for it may have had an important impact on the country's historical pace: Without these missionaries, would Russia have opened up as soon?

We often met at our house on Lenin Avenue for a big Russian dinner, with plenty of French wine and Russian vodka. We often went together to see friends. We went for long walks or rides in their car and we always had a great time together. Sometimes just Julia and I met for coffee and gossiped about men, her work, Moscow French. She generated the sharpest and the most vivid characteristics for people and phenomena I ever heard: Her definitions, descriptions, and jokes were individually colored and individually wrapped in the best of French linguistics. Julia brought to me excellent books, mostly mysteries and detective stories. She taught me how to appreciate the art and the language of that genre: from American and French classics to grotesque and hilarious parodies. I swallowed and digested them by the ton, like the Rabelaisian Gargantua, asking for more. Later in Paris Julia took me to a bookstore that specialized in detective, police, and mystery novels, where the owner, Julia's friend, gave me an assortment of books as a present. He could not believe I was from Moscow; not only did I speak without an accent, but I seemed to be at home in his store, with his books, their authors and characters. It felt like I had finally found the source, but its contents had been with me for a long time, maybe forever.

I made another intellectual discovery thanks to Marc and Julia. The cultural service of the French Embassy had a cinema program: French movies were shown a couple of times a week for the staff, but mostly with the goal of promoting French culture in the Soviet Union. Thanks to my friends, I always had a guest card. At the entrance of the Embassy, the Soviet policeman checked people's passports and often gave a very hard time to Soviet citizens, willing to be initiated into French culture. Those who cared about their jobs did not put themselves at risk; those who still did not want to believe in "Big Brother" were soon reminded by the presence of a KGB officer in their boss' office; those who had no career, had nothing to fear: they were free. That was the kind of freedom I had. Nevertheless, the "conversations" with the Soviet policemen were far from pleasant; there isalways an element of fear, the instinctive one, even if you do not have much to lose. After all, I had a family and a life.

Julia had a special taste, knowledge, and understanding of the cinema. We had long and exciting conversations about what I saw. I discovered Truffaut, Tavernier, Malle, Rivette, Vardas, Rhomer, Duras, Godard, Bunuel, and many others. I learned, as systematically as I could, the poetics of the cinema, its history, metaphor, and language. Authentic cinema, cinema as art, opened to me, developed my taste, and became, since then, one of my favorite leisuretime activities. And, of course, it was the best way to practice my listening comprehension skills. However, I never realized I was learning skills: I just enjoyed the movies! After a while, I forgot in which language I was watching them: I just enjoyed them, factually, emotionally, and intellectually.

I realize now that my friends were the best you can meet in any country: liberal intellectuals, low income non-conformist teachers, who had difficulties confronting their own reality. The meaning of the cultural messages I received from them in French, in any form or context, generated the language I was learning. Together, we spent a lifetime learning from each other, in mutual hope for a better world; with them, I fed myself with illusions about France; with me, they longed for our spirit in the Russian kitchens, away from their consumerist society.

They often told me that over the years of work in various college and university departments of Romance languages in Moscow and Leningrad, they had never met anybody like me, who spoke French without the slightest accent, who seemed to live, not just to know, French culture and civilization. I answered, "It is because nobody loves you as much as I do."

I cried very bitterly when they were leaving. The world seemed to be over. I knew I would never see them again: It was time for them to end their Russian adventures, to get settled in their own land, to have children, permanent work, a home. I would never, ever visit them, go through the iron curtain. Marc patted my hair, wiped my tears, and said, "You will. I promise you will." There was nothing in the stuffy Soviet air of that winter that smelled of spring.

But things started changing rapidly. One year after that farewell party, they came to meet me at La Gare du Nord, in Paris. Marc kept his word.

Christicha

Marie Christine (Christicha), like most foreign teachers on contract in Moscow, lived in the Moscow University Hotel, which offered a tiny room, with a tiny bathroom and no kitchen, for a 2- or 3-year stay. She taught inthe college I had graduated from, but as it usually happened in the Soviet Union, had no friends among her colleagues; everybody seemed hostile and unsociable. At that time she did not know that these people were just protecting their jobs, political reputations, and families; contacts with foreigners were fraught with all kinds of trouble. She was lonely in the foreign world which did not speak her language and where every little thing seemed overwhelmingly difficult.

Soon after we met and got close, I invited her to live with us for the summer. My husband's father usually moved out of town to his country house, his dacha, and we felt free, with a touch of teenage craziness, to do anything we wanted. Marie Christine was delighted: Not only could she stay with people she liked, but she could have normal meals, cook, go shopping, and share with us our household responsibilities. Her life "in the closet," as she called the hotel room, was driving her insane. She especially detested the "security guard" who was following her guests and requesting their passports, even when she wanted to sit with them in the lobby or go to the cafeteria. In anticipation of the fun of living together, we moved Christisha's belongings to our house. She unpacked and started to enjoy; she learned how to make the homemade cottage cheese that she loved, observed me cooking bortsch, and even added to our household a large German-made old plate with blue dragons and a ceramic bowl in which French have coffee with milk in the morning. I still have these precious gifts. For about a week we had all kinds of fun: from literature and poetry tea parties to long walks in the old Moscow. How happy we were to go back home together and expect my husband from work, who spoke some French and improved drastically with Christisha at home.

Once she called me and said, horrified and disgusted, "I have to go back to the hotel." She had been summoned to the office of the Dean who asked her a perfectly ethical question: "Where have you been sleeping over the last week?" He told her it was forbidden for her to stay anywhere else but in the hotel (where she could be watched) and mentioned my name, as an out-law promising trouble.

Friendship is particularly valued when the outside world is incomprehensibly hypocritical and hostile; it is the only connection to morality, the only force that reminds people that they are alive, the only link to human freedom and dignity. Christisha and I met as often as we could, even though she had to move back to the hotel in order to keep her job. She was the perfect woman friend. It was so easy to share with her the "female stuff," relationships, men, and gossip about my teachers—her colleagues and her French compatriots in Russia. There was something philosophical and at the same time therapeutic in her listening and feedback, and we often switched from these private themes to literary associations. The way she made me discover the best of contemporary French literature was through our exchange of personal experiences. I did not notice how it happened that her favorite authors and novels became my favorites: Marguerite Duras, Michel Tournier, Georges Pérec, Albert Cohen, Marguerite Yourcenar, Italo Calvino, and many others. It turned out it was our way to be together, to communicate via this literary language, and to relate to literature with our lives.

She told me, drinking her *thé alternatif* (which was by itself such a learning experience!), long fascinating stories about the *nouveau roman*, the concept of madness in durassian novels, and new feminist perspectives in French literature. She also made me acquainted with modern British, Italian, and German literature that I could read in French translation. She left me the books that had been the symbol of our friendship when she went back to France, and they remained forever the literary, intellectual, and personal treasures I always keep in my mind and on my shelves. Her language, impeccable and pure, was an example of literary orthoepic, lexical, and grammatical norm. She was the only French person I knew who did not use much slang, if any, and was always careful about the purity of her linguistic expression.

She specialized in classical languages, Latin and Greek, and French language and literature. Her hobby was theater: She gave a couple of lectures in Moscow about contemporary French theater, and I remember her confusion about how to present this topic to the Soviet audience who had never had a chance to see any French theater production. "It is like speculating and philosophizing about how certain food tastes. And what is even worse is that there is no hope to taste it," she used to tell me, expressing her frustration.

Our correspondence was not very regular, but we kept in touch: After her contract with Russia was over, Christisha went to Poland, where she got married and gave birth to her daughter, Sarah. She seemed to be happier in Poland, a country culturally closer to the western traditions, and adored her job and her family. When I visited her in Paris, at Monmartre, where she was on vacation, we took a long walk around that place so glorified in literature, had dinner at an outside cafe terrace, and browsed through the tiny bookstores, where she got for me *La Belle du Seigneur*, by Albert Cohen and some beautifully designed multicolored books for my little daughter.

When I reread some of the books we read and discussed together, I feel my friend is always with me, because this literature has spirit. Spirit can be expressed in a human language, but it cannot be perceived without human affinity.

Chapter 5

French Connection

There are certainly many writers and poets who entered my heart with their work—as did real people. Thanks to them, I am who I am not only as a physical and social survivor of systems, regimes, persecutions, and immigration, but, more importantly, as a human being in my relationship to others and self. Literature has made me feel at home—no matter what my reality was. French literature, with its intellectual and democratizing power, was especially meaningful in a totalitarian country, and I was eager to identify with it. It also created one of the most significant and effective inputs in my learning of French, in becoming fully functional in French, in acquiring a French identity. My initiation into the French culture via the free spirit of the medieval poetry of the scandalous François Villon, romantic Ronsard, stoicist Alfred de Vigny, the symbolists Baudelaire and Verlaine, modern surrealists, existentialists, and nouveau roman writers—this list is by no means inclusive—was the journey in space and time to my beloved France.

Those who inspired me and participated in the journey, my teachers and friends, were also the ones who made it technically possible. Books came from France with friends and through friends; they were borrowed, often for one night, or exchanged; my home French library was growing, including all genres and types, from the *romans de midinettes*, mysteries and their parodies to the contemporary novels of all movements and schools, and, of course, classics. The huge literary heritage of the French culture formed my thinking and feeling, and along with it—my use of the language. I could not think of French as a "foreign language"; it was not foreign, it was mine.

During my college years, through graduation, I had a group of friends with whom to share and reflect on these readings. It strikes me now that what is part of the educational system in the United States—literature or

English classes, workshops, seminars, and essay writing—was a natural, integrative part of our life. We never called it "education" or "learning," we did not see ourselves as "homemade scholars" or "self-educated professionals"—we just lived it. It was one of the elements of our intellectual and emotional salvation—that was what we did, that was what we were.

Most of us, including me, wrote and translated poems, songs, plays. We were the only judges of each other's creativity; it was absolutely unthinkable to have our pieces published or even seen by experts. The publishing and media sphere was heavily censored, controlled, and ideologized—our creation was free, inspired by western tradition, and out of heart: It did not belong to the Soviet market.

Maybe the only creative writing of mine ever read by an audience (college professors) was my master's thesis—a serious scholarly research project of about 100 pages, linking my linguistic and literary inclinations in the field of poetics—structural and formalistic in approach, marxist and comprehensive in form, poetic semiotic in content. This work was deeply rooted in my love of poetry and interest in versification, poetic translation, art, and the language of art. Its ultimate goal was to reveal the aesthetic essence of the poetic text, in other words to answer the essential question of poetics and aesthetics: What makes a piece of art? This research was a challenge almost impossible to fulfill in an ideologically limited framework, in the censored information supply, in tabooed scholarship. My work, based on the comprehensive analysis of a poem by Alfred de Vigny, emerged from the philosophy and methods of structuralism while the term *structuralism* was strictly forbidden; it examined the work of Vygotsky, Russian Formalists of the 1920s and 1930s, Tartu University's structural semioticians led by Yury Lotman—all these names and schools were heavily criticized. The thesis was written in French, strictly following the rules and discourse patterns of academic French. The research process was carefully guided, directed, and inspired by a remarkable scholar, author of numerous publications and books on French literature and poetics, professor Svetlana Yurievna Zavadovskaya, "Claire." My story of the impact of French literature on my growth as an individual and as a bilingual is simultaneously the story of people who brought it to me.

Coming from a Polish Russian aristocratic family of repatriates from France, which followed the bitter path of those from the west who believed in "building the communism," she suffered throughout her life and career from the stigma of the "bourgeois past." Claire (her French name) was an infinite source of knowledge and optimism and possessed a noble, aristocratic style of communication. Unlike her colleagues, she used to make friends with her favorite students (the "unfavorite" ones never made friends with her nor chose her as a research advisor) who felt at home in her house full of books and paintings by her husband, an artist, and with her old dog. In fact, the "staying with the dog experience" was one of the strongest intellectual encounters in my life; alone in Claire's house, I was free to read, to discover, to smell the world that I wanted so much to make my own. I guess I mistakenly associated French with the intellectual, sophisticated, noble, falling into the trap of a stereotype. The affinity we developed was the most important support for my research and later in my life. Claire thought that my scholarly and writing talents were very promising and predicted my future in scholarship. Naturally, I could not fit her predictions into my reality. After the brilliant thesis defense (held in French), I was recommended for a mark of distinction for my research and for a diploma cum laude. The dean of instructional services in charge of French studies, violently opposed this recommendation. His attacks were openly anti-semitic (against me) and anti-Zavadovskaya (against my advisor). The story of Claire's fight "as a tiger" for the deserved merits of her student and of the shameful behavior of the dean was told to me later. By that time I was not surprised nor humiliated by these attacks—living with them was a natural, almost biological part of my being. The dean could not defeat Claire and other faculty members who defended my work, but he found another way to take revenge; he arranged, through the examiners, that I would be given a "good," not the usual "excellent" grade for the French part of my Master's qualifying examinations. All the exams in Russia are orals, and there is no appeal procedure.

Professor Zavadovskaya was proud to recommend me for a doctoral program in the American university. Her recommendation letter, written in excellent English, is the symbol of the realization of her prediction and of my dream coming true.

Sometimes I believe that our stories repeat in a cycle or perhaps live in a nonlinear continuum. When I visit my present doctoral advisor at her home in Brooklyn, it smells like Claire's "artistic mess" of books, paintings, old pillows, and wood. The déjà vu continues in the dialogue, affinities, and academic matters. I simply trusted my feeling of vague recognition when I chose this wonderful woman—and I was right. By the way, I never called Svetlana Yurievna the informal "Claire": in this story it is probably the effect of the American déjà vu.

* * *

After graduation from college, I attempted to continue my research and wrote a long paper on the contrastive analysis of the versification principles in French and in Russian. This opus, among other manuscripts, had to be eliminated in the emigration preparations: the Soviet customs did not allow any manuscripts, without a special authorization, to be taken abroad. They made sure that we separated ourselves from everything and everybody that was dear, valuable, and sentimental. I remember that bonfire I made to burn packages and boxes of diaries and journals I had written since my early childhood, of letters, and manuscripts. I did it with a light heart—I knew that the most important manuscript I ever wrote in my home country was with me, in my mind, and this story is part of it. The little notebook with my poems, my Master's thesis, and the originals of our diplomas, that I was also prohibited to carry abroad, were trusted to the diplomatic mail of the Holland Embassy representing Israel; thanks to many people involved, they were returned to me in the United States.

* * *

One of the very special domains in the ocean of French cultural heritage I was "studying" was the traditional French Song, la Chanson and the chansonniers, continuing the medieval genre of the famous minstrels. Treasured records and tapes with the voices of Aristide Bruant, Edith Piaf, Jacques Brel, Georges Brassens, Georges Moustaki, and many others, including the most recent French rock, brought from the other side of the iron curtain were carefully exchanged and copied. But they were not only collected and listened to: One of the most difficult language tasks I ever accomplished was to transcribe the lyrics from the recordings. I used to spend hours on this job, trying to discern words from sounds and figure out the whole song. Sometimes it appears difficult even in a native language! Rewinding—playing; rewinding— playing, hundreds of times; using the dictionary, using the brain, associating, generalizing, guessing—until the meaning and the sounds come together.

Lyrics are extremely important in French songs; they are the essence of the half musical, half poetic rhythmic genre. I took tremendous pleasure in the process of deciphering as a poetic experience; I also enjoyed the satisfaction of a eurica, once a difficult song was done. Later I transcribed lyrics from English and Italian songs for my husband's music band. I always found this listening comprehension practice greatly important for my language skills. However, the linguistic exercise in itself was not my primary motivation: what really stimulated me is that I felt part of the culture. I often attempted to translate French songs into Russian.

We sang our favorite songs with the guitar at parties, picnics or trips. We, "The French Company," a group of students specializing in French studies, were the main organizers and creators of various college extracurricular activities: concerts, thematic parties, amateur performances. I often wrote play scripts for these events and sang, recited, acted on stage. We had fun—and we learned and created. That is what real learning must be about.

French culture, which in its various forms brought about the authentic revolutionary spirit, substituted for us the spiritual emptiness in the country of the "winning revolution." This liberating spirit united us, young people, always in search of justice, our heads full of illusions and hope, and offered us common grounds for special relationships and unique friendships. The intellectual and spiritual values we shared around common "French inter-ests" made us close and free of prejudice. Interestingly enough, most of my friends of that time have found their own self-actualization in our difficult postmodernist changing world; the nexus of the group is leading one of the most democratic radio stations in the politically eclectic and almost anar-chic Moscow of today; some of us have moved to Europe, some—to America. All of us have become somebody. If my old friends could hear me now, I would only whistle the famous Brassens's tune, the anthem of our France and friendship, *Les Copains d'abord*—and they would turn their heads and be back.

Georges Brassens, the classic of the French Song, a chansonnier, poet, philosopher, musician, and bard, has been our common and my personal idol and guru. His songs were the most difficult to transcribe because they represented a sophisticated mixture of French folklore, Latin and Gallic spirit, romantic and symbolic poetry, profanities, sarcasm, Céline's existen-tialism, Greek and Roman mythology—all in a blend of styles, discourses, and archaisms, including Old French. Brassens was the messenger of Villon and Ronsard, Flaubert and Hugo, Valéry and Baudelaire. He was challeng-ing modern French society, scandalizing the *petit bourgeois*, questioning the existing moral and religious values, and calling for the authenticity of feelings and words. As many poets of our time, Brassens expressed his alienation from his own cultural socium—and that is what we, Soviet students, found so attractive. Brassens was never translated in the Soviet Union, thus he was absolutely unknown. Only in the 1980s were two or three of his songs published in a translation of Bulat Okudjava, a poet, writer, and bard of the similar dimension in Russia. Right before my emigration, I wrote a preface for the book *Masters of French Song* in cooperation with a friend, a music journalist. I never saw the book and never got paid for the work. But I was happy to write about Brassens, among other chansonniers, and I considered it an honor to contribute to his memory and popularization. His strong poetic and human spirit accompanied my difficult years in Russia, immigration, and my difficult transition to a new life in America. The old, fringed, dog-eared poster with a rough mustached man in his 60s, a pipe in his mouth and the guitar in his hands, was the only home decoration on the empty walls of our first unfurnished apartment in New York. I was told that a poster of Brassens is impossible to get now in France; the immortal poets do not belong to consumer fashion—they belong to eternity.

Chapter 6

Language Acquisition by Stomach

It's only after I've taken in disparate bits of cultural matter, after I've accepted its seductions and its snares, that I can make my way through the medium of language to distill my own meanings; and it's only coming from the ground up that I can hit the tenor of my own sensibility, hit home.
> —Eva Hoffman, *Lost in Translation*

The Dandelion Salad

Once—it was in early May, when the warm caressing sun turns Moscow into light and greenness, and Muscovites seem to thaw like the ice in the streets after a long and gloomy winter—my French friend Marie Christine asked me if I would agree to offer my place for her birthday party at my home because her hotel room was too small to receive guests. She said that she would get the food and cook a real Breton dinner for her French and Russian friends. I was delighted with the idea.

At that time there was a terrible food shortage that became worse every day. One would go shopping to get whatever was available, and with some luck they would bring home "food," anything that could make a meal. Marie Christine, like most of my French friends, wanted to be immersed in the total cultural experience and patiently tried to live a "normal Soviet life," which included, among other things, food hunting, standing on long lines, cleaning soiled vegetables, and preparing homemade cottage cheese. Sometimes she got impatient, gave up the *couleur locale*, and traveled by subway to shop at the French Embassy store or to a *Beriozka*, a foreign currency store. In my eyes the option to do that reversed her "cultural efforts" to some kind of artificially inflicted masochism. I was convinced then that the privileges given to foreigners in the Soviet Union, including food provision, made their cultural—and along with it, linguistic—assimilation practically impossible.

The "capitalist decay" smelled great! *Beriozka* provided Marie Christine with foods never seen in my apartment: salami, smoked ham, olives, hazelnuts, different kinds of cheeses, French wine, and many other things we had only read about. The entrée was a Breton specialty, real Quiche Lorraine. But the salad my French friend intended to serve turned into a poetic adventure. First we had to pick dandelions at a nearby park, situated next to Moscow University. Without a touch of a smile, Marie Christine explained to us that dandelion leaves are good to eat only when they are very young, in the early spring, and instructed which ones were good, which ones were not. The Russians traditionally pick mushrooms and berries in the woods—out of their historical poverty—but nobody ever saw people picking dandelions in a Moscow park! We had lots of fun looking at each other, hands and bags full of dandelions and joking about the "poor French" who ate for special occasions what even "poor Russians" did not consider edible. We finally agreed that the French were definitely very extravagant. Marie Christine soaked the leaves in cold water, then chopped them, and mixed them with fried ham and croutons, cheese, and hazelnuts. The salad was served with a homemade sauce vinaigrette. It was a great success although the opinion of the Russian guests' was that with such exquisite ingredients, the salad would be as good without dandelions!

French Cheeses and Science Fiction

Any well-read person knows how important cheeses are in France. French literature is always explicit about the meals, foods, wines, restaurants, cafés, bistros—all these attributes that make French literature a colorful, authentic, and delicious analogue of culture. But what becomes of taste or smell when it is only a word? What happens if the reading has no real experiential association? When we read about nature—sun, rain, trees, flowers—we can mentally picture the description that has our knowledge about it to rely on. When we read about people, we are given freedom to imagine them. But the basic, nonexotic foods or beverages described in the literature, are not science fiction objects because they really exist and are available in any supermarket.

For a Soviet reader, though, all the food descriptions, among other western "artifacts," called for a tremendous work of imagination and in many cases seemed absurd or ridiculous. For example, are the French crazy to eat that dried up, yucky thing (the equivalent of most Soviet cheeses) *after* dinner, for dessert? Or: is Hemingway's famous "double frozen daiquiri" some green liquid stuff with a double portion of ice? How do you serve green lettuce salad to your guests if the lettuce is mostly yellow, soiled, and as dead as Prévert's *feuilles d'automne*? Not to mention the infinite number of foods' and dishes' names unheard of, representing either fish or meat and becoming exotic words deprived of meaning. Even reading Russian literature classics at Brezhnev times was a culinary science fiction experience: Foods and recipes disappeared with their names—and the whole culture got afflicted with amnesia!

French cheeses, four or five brands, were triumphantly served on a traditional straw plate, with a traditional bifurcated knife for the New Year dinner by my friends Mireille and Marie Neige, who were in Moscow for their winter vacation. Once smelled and tasted, the literary images had to fit into a too tight Soviet reality, to debunk the myth created by food shortages and cultural isolation.

Sometimes I want to forget the past, just let it go—but I cannot forgive "them" for what they did to Russian culture that might be, in a historical scope, an irreversible process. The example of the cuisine is only the minimal damage, but the humiliation of people obliged to "mentally taste," "mentally smell," and reinvent in their minds various foods, invented by the civilization long ago, is also irreversible. At least, for me.

Noel

Domka was busy with Christmas party preparations: she took her own idea very seriously—not only because she knew she was accomplishing a mission of cultural involvement and sharing, but I think mostly because she was not a gifted cook, not a *cordon bleu*. We both spent hours reading the French cook book, trying to figure out which recipes were "doable." We rejected one dish after another because there were always ingredients missing: either herbs non-existent even in *Beriozka*, or a kind of oil, or nuts. Finally we gave up and decided to cook whatever was easiest: *gratin aux pommes-de-terre*, crab salad, *julienne de champignons*. Domka also wanted to serve various kinds of smoked meat and salami, the *charcuterie*.

The day of the feast, December 24, she showed up at my place, late and frozen to death, with white frostbitten cheeks and red fingers. I had known her for many years, and I knew that winter, especially Russian winter, was not her favorite season! What was it that made her stay out in the icy wind for so long? The answer was in her hands: it was a huge package with grayish salami. It turned out that on her way to my house she saw a big line of people and "smelled something good." She found out it was salami! Oh great, great luck: She would get salami for her Christmas dinner! Before she stood on this line, Domka, like other foreigners, had never understood why the Russians always bought things in huge amounts. It certainly was not because they ate too much! With every small movement of the line forward she was increasing the amount of salami she would buy. By the time it was finally her turn (3 hours later) she decided to get 2 kilos, even though she needed one tenth of it for the party. I complimented my friend on her successful acculturation.

Chapter 7

My Italian Self

Ma chère Marie Christine,

Buongiorno dall'Italia! Come stai?

Did you know that the American Jewish philanthropic organizations had founded the transit centers for Eastern European Jews in Vienna, Austria, and in Rome, Italy, as early as in the 30s? Interestingly enough, both countries were fascist. Thus, we are following the historical road to America, the pilgrimage to freedom. Here in Italy, we are applying for our entrance visa to America. We are supposed to wait for the interview with the American Consul and meanwhile rent a place to live somewhere close to Rome. We settled in Santa Marinella, a small resort town near Rome, a charming place on the sea shore. If we were not here for a difficult transition from one world to another with all the imlications of it, I would think we are here for a "Rome vacation," except that we are broke.

Dear Marie Christine, you won't believe it, after everything you saw in Russia and after you witnessed the horrors of our exodus, but the terrifying rumors about the change in the American immigration policy toward the Russian Jews seem to be correct:

Thousands of our people, assisted by Jewish phi-
lanthropies, are stuck in Italy, lost between two
worlds and overwhelmingly confused. Nobody knows
for how long this situation will last and who and
by which law will make it to America. Through the
grapevine I heard that Israel is putting a lot of
pressure on the American government and is attempting to "buy our souls."

Meanwhile, I am learning Italian. I think it will
help me out whatever happens to us, and the only
thing that really worries me is my poor parents'
arrival to this political mess. As usual, politics
has nothing to do with human lives—this is our first
discovery about the western world. I think that we
had fed ourselves for so long with illusions about
justice simply because its lack in the Soviet Union
had made us assume its existence in the opposite
part of the world. Even my constant and close
contacts with you and the other westerners had never
made me beware. I guess I heard only what I wanted
to hear. How naive!

But that is not what I wanted to write about.
The situation, like in Russia, is out of our
control at this point—so we had better enjoy
Italy. I immediately thought about you, as my
literary advisor, when we got to this place.
Civita Vecchia, made famous by Stendhal, is only
half an hour of drive from where we are. By the
way, we are moving around by hitchhiking: It seems
a normal way to go to places for the Italians.
Not only do they find it absolutely safe and
harmless, but often stop to treat us with coffee
or a snack. They seem to be as adventurous as we
are, looking for company and a nice chat while
driving—I can maintain some conversation fairly
well now and even tell them our complicated story
of the why, where, and how of emigration.
Sometimes I have to travel just by myself, and I

never feel insecure in the car with men. Once they begin flirting, I tell them I am not interested—and they stop right away. Is this a result of the *éducation sentimentale* of this romantic culture or the impact of Catholicism?

I cannot believe that everything I read about becomes alive. The Soviet system made us wonder about the fact of the existence of the outside world and made us create a fantasy, out of readings and pictures. Things existed, smelled, and tasted only mentally—my God! What did they do to us?

So, Stendhal's Civita Vecchia and Marguerite Duras' Tarquinia! I know there is much more in the real world, but when I saw those Etruscan horses in Tarquinia, from your and my favorite novel *Les Petits Chevaux de Tarquinia* in this ancient, millenia-old town and fortress, I suddenly realized what Duras is saying in her book! Her characters, wealthy French vacationers, spending their long and dull "existential" vacation in a little Italian town (was it Santa Marinella?), drinking bitter campari and spending long hours at the beach, are striving to the ultimate goal, only a couple of miles away: to see these Etruscan little horses carved in wood. Like many of Chekhov's characters longing to go "to Moscow," they have created a fantasy of the real and physically close world. Think about it, chère amie: I made it in the opposite direction, from very far away in the social equivalent of miles or kilometers, from a fantasy imposed on me—to the reality.

Dear Marie Christine, it is time to say good-bye now. Pavel and Pauline send you their love. See you in this part of the world!

Bises,

Natacha.

➢ ➢ ➢

Caro Alberto!

I find it a wonderful ritual of yours—to send us postcards from everywhere you go: now, as back in Moscow, I enjoy these "Baci" from Sweden, Switzerland, England, and France. I cannot afford to travel now, as I hoped I would once I become a free American. I am busy building my new life: *à la guerre comme à la guerre*!

We always remember you: your visits to Moscow which always turned into feasts and your prompt and kind participation in our destiny when we were refused the American refugee visa in Italy. I will never forget your explicit and powerful letter to the American Consul testifying about our political situation in Russia. Your charming invitations for dinners and tours in Rome were not less appreciated. Alberto, we always greatly valued your kindness and generosity which we will never be able to repay. I sense, from my understanding of the Italian culture, that friendship is perceived as the most precious gift—so it is by the Russians. Is it the warmth, the openness, and the hospitable spirit of your country that made Italian "an easy language" to learn?

Apropos, I have to answer your question about my Italian. Yes, I took some basic Italian in college, not more than 15 or 20 hours all in all, but never really used it. I never had a chance to speak, read, and write before our 6-month stay in Italy as transit émigrés. I had studied Latin though, in college. It was a required course for my major and it turned out to be an extremely thorough and profound study, two semesters long. I excelled in it. I admired the systematicity that language represents and the beauty of the logic where linguistic elements and relationships are interconnected, creating grammatical and syntactic meaning. Yes, Latin made me admire the language form—maybe that was my first exposure to structuralism? My boyfriend (*canis doctus*) and I (*avis rara*) amused ourselves talking in Latin: it was a funny exercise which evoked mathematic operations, not meaning making. As a scientist, you must understand what I mean.

When we were packing for our unexpectedly long trip through Europe to America, I took an Italian textbook with me. It was a conservative, typical Soviet text, based on translation, with the stories about *camarada Lorenzo*, member of the Italian Communist Party. Even so, I appreciated the book because it contained a lot of grammar materials, thorough explanations of the grammar and syntactic forms and their usage. I used to read the rules every day on the train on my two hour trip to Rome from Santa Marinella, and the same thing at night, back to Santa Marinella from work. During the day, I listened and absorbed the sounds, words, grammar forms, intonations, gestures. I amused myself with a mental game, sort of puzzle: following the "rules of the game," I would try to form tenses, irregular forms, participles—and in most cases I did it correctly. It was a fascinating game for a linguist, which consisted of reconstructing or reinventing the language according to Latin, French, and English linguistic rules, my general knowledge, and sense of orientation in Romance linguistics, and of course the famous "feel" for a language. My intuition was my training, my creativity with the Italian grammar and vocabulary was the reality of my contact with languages.

I remember, you and I had a discussion about Italian domestic politics over coffee in a train station café—it was my second or third month of stay in Italy. I was surprised myself to be able to do it in Italian, but I enjoyed it so much that I was willing to take the risks of the ridiculous mistakes by acting out being Italian. I guess you can do it only when you really like your role, and

I was truly in love with Italy. When you complimented me by calling me Ornella Mutti, I really wondered whether a mistake had been made about the place of my birth.

I will never forget, Alberto, the wonderful Italians I met, and you among them, of course. It was not only a pleasure, but an emotional need to speak to them in their language to repay their hospitableness, to understand them and their life to the roots, to feel adequately and at home. My "home" was the language.

Thank you, dear Alberto, for your nice invitation. I will certainly take advantage of it when the time comes, and visit you and the dolce paese, la casa mia.

Please write. *Molti, molti baci,*

Natasha.

≻ ≻ ≻

Cara Signora Begnini, caro Paolo—

When I heard about the elimination of HIAS[1] in Rome, I immediately thought about you. Unfortunately I lost track of you a couple of years ago, and now I feel the need to go back in time and space and locate you two in the world. I am wondering where you are, what you are doing, where are you working now, after HIAS "went out of business?" Perhaps S-ra Begnini has retired and is finally having some rest, after years of energy-draining work. Please write. I would be so happy to keep in touch!

As you already know, we are quite settled in America. I am teaching English to immigrants in college, and my husband is a social worker. I often go back to Italy in my mind and think about you, my work at HIAS, my struggle for an American refugee visa, and your gentle presence in my transitional

---

[1]HIAS is the Hebrew International Aid Society

life. I owe you two my infinite gratitude for being
greatly human, and I am convinced that you happened
to be at the right place at the right time serving
refugees, "lost souls." You made a difference in
their confused lives.

Interestingly enough, I chose to continue the
work You, S-ra Begnini, had started in Rome many
years ago, when you and a group of Italians had
founded a resettlement agency to help Eastern
European Jews to change their lives. I also work
here in the U.S. with people who, like me, are
making a difficult cultural, emotional, and linguistic transition: I help them to acquire a new
language—I am a linguist, I am a teacher. But I
am something else to my students: I am also their
counselor and sometimes a friend. My work experience in Rome, beside you, helped me to understand
the importance of the emotional and psychological
factors in the emigre reality and how this human
sphere can be dealt with. I strongly believe that
we can assist our students to adjust to a new life
via "language therapy"—and vice versa, learn the
language via reality. We have to respect their life
and struggle, like you taught me by your personal
example.

Thanks to many little signs of attention and
friendliness you showed me, such as treating me
with ice-cream during the lunch break or giving me
an encouraging smile, along with your invaluable
assistance in my appeal process, I felt relieved
of the feeling of being unwanted, rejected, and
humiliated. Thanks to you, I never transferred my
anger to Italy—as my parents did—and even on the
contrary, embraced its refuge as a friend's home,
a hospitable environment of affection and friendship. I must thank you and your son again and again
for your support.

Dear Paolo, you asked me at my farewell party in
the office how I felt about the whole of my Italian

experience, including my family's hardships of
everyday survival and the bitterness of my first
encounter with the western world. I was too
overwhelmed and confused then to give you a
satisfactory answer; I was torn between my parents'
unhappiness and my happiness living in your country; I was trying to reason pragmatically about
where immigration is "easier." Perhaps now, years
later, I am able to formulate a plausible answer.

Every morning, after I got off the train, and
walked for 20 minutes to the office at via Regina
Margerita, I sniffed the Rome morning aroma of
capuccino, latte machiato, pastry, and fresh bread,
smiled at smiling back Italian faces, exchanged the
ritualistic ciao with the coffee shop waiter where
I read my French newspaper and an article or two
from the Italian one. Every morning I could not
believe that it was really happening to me, that I
could touch century-old stones, see Fellini's urban
landscapes right from the office window—and be part
of the movie! Paolo, I have to admit now that I
carefully "overheard" all your phone conversations,
trying to make your speech my own. My language
learning was an exciting adventure! By the time I
was able to speak Italian at work, which I insisted
on doing even though almost everybody in HIAS spoke
English, to make business phone calls, to live a
surrogate of normal life—my fight with the American
consulate was over: I won and had to leave again,
to start everything over, make another home. And
even the little vacation to Venice and Florence we
took before leaving Italy, more of a theatrical
than life experience, could not overshadow in
emotional force my everyday routine in Rome. Real,
authentic life versus tourist experience, with its
culture, people, and language, always so difficult
to touch in a foreign country, is the most
fascinating thing. I am sure that the knowledge
this experience of close contact with language and

culture generates makes people intellectually
richer and more humane—kinder, more open, sympathetic and friendly. By embracing the culturally
diverse human experience, we become better people.
You certainly did, Paolo. And this is the answer
to your question.

This is my way to say thank you once again. God
bless you both, all Begnini family, and hope to see
you again.

Ciao,

Natasha.

➢ ➢ ➢

Caro Mario,

Saluti da New York!

I hope you and Maria are in good health, and your
children and grandchildren live happy and successful lives. This is what I always pray for.

How does Santa Marinella look now? What's new in
town? As far as I know, the "Russian invasion" of
Santa Marinella is over, after the immigration
policy has changed. Now the Russian Jews apply for
their American refugee visas in Moscow and travel
directly to the United States. Certainly, it makes
it easier for everybody, but think about what they
are missing!

What is her name, Santa Marinella's real estate
agent who must have made a fortune on us? I also
forgot the bartender's name, from the Bar Centrale
next to the train station where the telephone was?
I forgot many names of people and places, but I
will never forget yours. Pauline says she will
always remember you. You know, she calls herself
Paula now, the Italian way. Of course she remembers

mostly the ice cream and chewing gum that miraculously appeared in your hand as soon as she showed
up outside. She always asks me how it was possible
that you were always there when she got out of the
house. I told her that you were *always* there for
us. I still think that you offered my husband a job
as your assistant because you did not see any other
way to make us accept your money—you fed us
physically, morally, and spiritually. How can I
forget those fresh eggs *per bambini* and *la verdura*,
pizza, and homemade grappa for grown-ups? And the
big family dinners, with *pizza dal forno al legno*,
with women serving, feeding, cleaning—in honor of
my parents, lost between the worlds? Maria was
shaking her head: *molto preoccupati*.… At that time
the town was full of rumors about suicides and heart
attacks out of despair and extreme frustration all
over the Russian settlement area. I know that you
were aware of it, and you did everything you could
to ease our tension.

But how could we communicate if I had not learned
some Italian? How could I express my gratitude,
explain our situation, or let Pauline play with
your granddaughter? How would we understand that
one has cappuccino only in the morning, and
espresso—in the afternoon or evening? We admired
your culture, in its simplest, basic, and most
authentic norms of village life, and we accepted
your generosity, as natural as *la verdura* from your
garden.

I will never forget your presence and your car,
always available to move us from house to house,
and your desire to initiate us to the essence of
your life: from food to the religious happening of
Easter (*La Pasqua*). You took us with you, and we
moved with the crowd of villagers from place to
place to watch the biblical scenes of life and death
of Jesus, acted out in the streets' scaffolds, on
the roads, on the mountain, in the field. It was

the best theater I ever went to! During the season of the masquerades, we went together to the joyous parades, to see the laughing and singing crowds of villagers in bright costumes. For Christmas, *Il Natale*, there was another home reception: you did not want to admit that we would stay alone that happy night at our miserable home. And of course there were Christmas presents.

Dear Mario, your need for sharing helped us feel like insiders, not outsiders of your life and transformed our pain into force.

Maybe that was the most important incentive to speak your language: to be able to say thank you, *grazie, molto grazie*, Mario!

Is Santa Marinella sleepy and quiet, back to normal, with its usual rhythm of markets on Wednesdays, summer vacationers from Rome, sunny white houses and villas on the slope of the mountain? There are no more signs in Russian in the grocery stores ("This is not sour cream!"), no noisy meetings at the sea shore, and no lines at the post office. Sometimes I want to go back to Santa Marinella to make sure this place really existed at the crossroad of two histories and cultures, two languages, and two families.

Mario, are You really there?

God bless You.

Natasha.

The author's father's family, circa 1932, Ukraine. The two children in the front are Natasha's father, Yury (right) and his brother Georgui (left); their parents, Yulia and Yakov (above left). Yulia's parents and her brother are to the right.

The author's mother's family, circa 1947, Moscow. Natasha's mother, Yeva Novik with her sister, Ilia and their parents, Yefim and Mina.

Natasha's parents in 1949, on their honeymoon in Leningrad (Saint Petersburg).

Natasha at 9 in the elementary school.

Natasha in college, Moscow 1977.

Natasha (fifth from right) with her French class at the Moscow Language Center, French Poetry Night, 1986.

An evening among close friends; Marc (second on the left) with his wife Julia (behind Marc); next to Marc is Domka.

Natasha, crying on Marc's shoulder the evening in 1987 that he and his wife were leaving Moscow.

Natasha arriving at La Gare du Nord in Paris, 1988. This was her first time out of the iron curtain.

Natasha, her husband Paul and their daughter Pauline in Santa-Marinella, Italy, 1989, during their transition from Russia to the United States. Pauline is holding the little stuffed mouse in her hands.

Natasha, teaching ESL at Kingsborough Community College, 1993.

Natasha, 7 months pregnant at the pregraduation meeting in 1995 held by the Union Institute doctral committee members. Committee members are (from left to right) Dr. Roni Natov, Dr. Susan Roos, Pat Joice, Dr. Cindy Greenberg, and Dr. Rebecca Mlynarczyk.

Natasha with her friends—all colleagues from Kingsborough (Jared, Tara, and Paula) celebrating Natasha's PhD in 1995.

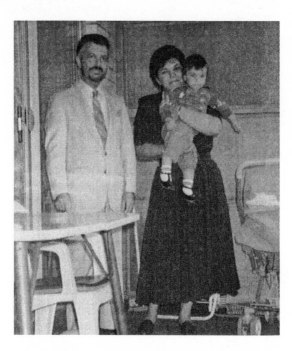

Natasha, Paul, and Julia (15 months old) in 1996.

Chapter 8

The American Diary

My first day in America. Brooklyn. An apartment like you would see in any suburban area of Moscow, where the elderly live—this apartment belongs to friends of my parents. It is in Brighton Beach. I don't understand television: the voices seem deep and guttural, only separate words reach my mind. I am tired and sleepy. We are all half alive, after the 10 hour flight from Italy. The urban landscapes on our way from JFK airport to Brooklyn are ugly: I cannot believe that is my reality now. I am depressed already.

I miss Italy, my homeland, the dolce paese! I did not realize then that our stay in Rome was a "Rome vacation" after all, and I was Audrey Hepburn, so familiar to me from her part of Natasha Rostov in the American version of Tolstoi's War and Peace—what a coincidence! But my vision of America had never been like Audrey's pretty face. Neither was it like Brooklyn. It is the place to escape to, where the Jews are free, from where there is no place to go farther, a geographic dead end.

From my Italian experience I have no illusions about social justice in America: Since August 1988, when the Soviet Jews' role in the political trade between the Soviet and American politicians ceased to be a product of exchange, human lives did not count anymore. Caught in the trap in Italy, without documents, money, and identity, with all our lives, families, and values left behind, and with four suitcases of belongings generously allowed by the Soviet customs to be taken abroad, we were refused refugee status by the American

*government even though we had spent years struggling with the
Soviet regime to obtain exit visas. America was the only visible help
back in Russia, the only place where we felt we were wanted—and
suddenly it all turned wrong. We were stuck in Italy, between two
chairs; no way to go back and no way to move forward. Our first
lesson of what America really is was very bitter. I know how deeply
it affected my parents who since then have never accepted America.
I think that I hate America.*

~ ~ ~

*Yes, I do! God, how ugly, these apartment buildings in Brooklyn! How
dirty these streets are! Definitely so: what had been a promised land
for the last generation, becomes a prison for the next!*

*We are looking for a place to rent. We only have the money for 1
month rent deposit, from our savings in Italy. We quickly understand
that NYANA, the Jewish philanthropic organization assisting Russian
Jews in New York, does not provide enough to rent a decent place.
How are we going to survive? To which school can we send our
daughter? What will I do when my English is not their English?*

~ ~ ~

*We have finally rented a pretty, apartment, which is too expensive for
us. The subway is so close it seems to live there with us. I can't help
recalling Woody Allen's autobiographical movie where his childhood
apartment at Coney Island shakes each time the train passes. It is
very funny in the movie. It is not very funny in reality. I cannot hear
well on the phone, so I have to close the windows in order to be able
to talk.*

*Oh the damn phone! I have so much to do, for all the family, to try
to solve their immediate problems—and all of this is done over the
phone. I know exactly what I should say and how I should say it, but
it does not sound right, something is missing. Each time I have to
speak English on the phone, I force myself, I hate myself, but I do it.
I never liked English. I had to learn it because it was compulsory in
school and after that—because this is the language spoken in America. It always sounded so harsh, so foreign as if there was no feeling*

*in it, no connection to human reality. Except—when I was reading
"Gone with the Wind" a couple of years ago, I felt something, I felt
the beauty!*

~ ~ ~

*The apartment we have rented smells familiar: There was a bookcase
in the living room, full of books, when we first walked in; there is nice,
warm, pastel colored wallpaper in the kitchen, with pictures of pots
and jars; the floor is shining parquet, and everything is clean—so
human, so homelike. The owner is a college English teacher, perhaps
a well-read person, extremely tactful and gentle, but I have no time
nor enough English to find out more. I know there is something he
left in this apartment—and that is the spirit, the home ghost who
smells of the owner's life. I do not know at this point what it is, but I
am grateful.*

*We have a bed, and my daughter sleeps on a cot we borrowed from
friends. I put the poster of Brassens on the wall—this is home. My
husband washes dishes in a nearby Russian restaurant all day and
comes back with his hands white and swollen—a heartbreaking
picture. I want to cry when I see his hands, but I can't. I have no tears.
We can pay the next month's rent now!*

~ ~ ~

*We have received some money from NYANA for the furniture. Instead,
we get ourselves a television set, a video cassette recorder, and some
audio equipment: my husband can listen to his jazz now, I can play
my French music, and we watch television—every day, hour after
hour. My husband uses the headphones and actually understands
English better and better. I stare at the colored screen, like one in a
trance, immersed in disgust over the television programs and the
content of the news. Is there anything more intellectual to see? Is this
a country of nonintellectuals? Are they trying to immerse people in
some kind of trance, so that they will stop thinking and feeling? I try
not to let my anger take hold of me, but I know it is there, powerful,
black, and blinding. I understand almost 80% of television now.*

The apartment looks funny, with all this home equipment and a bed—that is all we have. It does not bother me at all, but what bothers me is my depression, hatred, anger, sense of disorientation. Isn't this the place where by definition you can do the most important things you were not able to do back there? Isn't the American myth alive?

~ ~ ~

I've got a job! Even though I did not understand half of what the director was saying to me, I pretended I did. A friend of a friend recommended me for an English as a second language (ESL) teaching position in a business school. What is a business school? How can it be private if the students are not paying a cent? Why is the ESL program there? What is this whole thing about? How can we all survive on my $13 an hour, which is twice as much as the dish-washing salary, but still not enough to feed three people. What are "benefits"? What does it mean, "no benefits"???

~ ~ ~

Every morning I take the subway to go to work. I sit there with my player on, French songs in the headphones. My ears are closed—and my eyes go blind. This is salvation. Sometimes I see all kinds of people around; they are all so different from Europeans, and they speak in different languages I don't understand. How can they all be so different? Hasidic Jews in last century outfits, women in wigs and weird round hats—are they the people I can identify with? Do they come from the world of persecution and antisemitism? No, they look perfectly happy, they have no personal memories of what it means to be Jewish in Europe. They are perfect strangers, like everybody else in the street, in the subway car, in the school where I am teaching. My recent experience alienates me from everybody. I am Russian here, not Jewish. But am I Russian like other Russians in Brighton Beach? I am different from them, too. So I go to the French bookstore on Fifth Avenue—what a relief! Just touching these books and records is home.

~ ~ ~

I will never get used to this work environment! Who are these people?
They are not competent, their language and jokes are so rough, their eyes
are empty, and there is something wrong in their business. Everything is
nonprofessional, and the administration are crooks. But what exactly is
going on? I have no idea. I just work, get my paycheck, and go back home
to look for a real job—there should be something out there that would
make my dreams come true! Sometimes I hate the students also because
I hate this stuffy place where you freeze in the winter and choke in the
summer, no windows, no air, no air, no air....

With every class module I teach I feel I can really teach English.
The more I teach, the more I learn, the more I understand about that
language. The level of students does not require sophistication; they
are mostly beginners, and I play by ear about how to teach them. I
discover more and more about the actual usage of grammar, not
about grammar, about the context for vocabulary usage, not the
vocabulary, and I remember so well the idioms used by real people,
and the appropriateness of slang. I like it much more now that it is
real.

Yes, I like it. I pretend I have known all this all my life, and I teach
my students what I just learned from a conversation with a janitor
during the break. Language becomes my own when I teach it to the
students, and I really enjoy that moment. I guess the meaning, in all
its depth—that comes from life, not from words. I feel how blank
words are for the students. I never experienced that with French,
perhaps because I had been hearing and seeing the language used
for so long. Often, I don't know such simple English words as broom
or staples; it is because I never needed them! But I can easily
communicate on sophisticated subjects because so many French
words are borrowed into English to mean abstract concepts and for
characterization as adjectives. I sound very sophisticated then. I have
a hard time with purely Germanic root words and with prepositions
in the two-word verbs. When I grasp the system, I learn how to play
that up–down–back–on–off–over game. I enjoy it.

~ ~ ~

I am a linguist. What difference does it make for a linguist, which
language to learn, which language to teach? I can enjoy the process

of constructing the language, mentally building rules and systems, taking notes of irregularities, and admiring—yes, admiring the beauty of the linguistic logic. I know I am learning. I am learning very fast, all by myself, like an experienced linguist should do, like I always did. I am learning from people around me, from shopping, from office signs, and from my own teaching. I am learning from trying to become once again what I have always been: a linguist.

~ ~ ~

The French Consulate on Fifth Avenue. I spoke to the attaché of the "Service Linguistique," spent hours in their library with the directories of French companies and services. But what can I do except speak French like all these people do? I have no other skills, and they don't need translators!

The United Nations, French and Russian departments: I must go back to the Soviet Union to take the UN interpreter test? No way! Bilingual personnel employment agencies—who needs a multilingual secretary with the snobbism of a European education and a background in linguistics, literature, and poetics? No typing, no computer skills—French and Russian poetry!

Other employment agencies: from the ones assisting refugees to "how-would-you-like-your-coffee?" for executives. Wrong. All wrong. But how do you know what is right or wrong unless you explore and find out?

Translation bureaus: Do I want to translate technical and legal documents? Do I have a computer and fax machine?

Resumés, cover letters, new resumés, booklets on the job search. What a great language learning experience, of all styles and types of discourse! Sometimes I feel I have been writing these letters of application all my life. I enjoy it as a linguistic exercise. I think that I can write all kinds of things now because I have the feel. Friends come to consult me. I've got an electronic typewriter, with memory and a tiny display. This machine is a miracle, and I type and retype hundreds of letters and resumés. I also study the help wanted section in The New York Times. Since I have to get the thick newspaper on Sundays, I read it all—I love its style! It takes me months to comprehend the system of advertising jobs, its language, slang, and acronyms. It takes me more months to learn how and when to respond. What a frustration was the discovery of a separate page with jobs in education, after long months of job search! I almost feel I want to give up. I keep the "refusal" or "thank-you–no-thank-you" letters in a box, and the pile is growing and growing. Something is wrong, but I won't find out unless I do it. So I do it, ferociously, angrily, almost madly.

~ ~ ~

Universities, MLA job lists—what does "adjunct" mean? Do I want to teach a 4-hour course in Russian literature in Nevada? What will my husband do there? My parents will not manage without me.

"Voice of America," BBC, Monterey Foreign Language Institute, applications, oral and written exams, great scores, interviews, correspondence, but no jobs. Do I really want all that? A contract with the BBC, but what about my family? I feel that it is not an adventure anymore, not a Rome or Paris vacation. It's life. It's real. We need food, medical insurance, schooling for my daughter, new clothes, and a lot of care for my parents. I have to be realistic. I must be responsible. It is not a joke anymore.

~ ~ ~

Something is missing in my way of functioning in English. Something substantial, important, which does not let me enjoy my linguistic performance. It is like I am floating on the surface of the ocean, giving curious glances into its depth. It's like I am fishing for a deeper essence, and sometimes I get some fish, but they are separate fishes, not the overall picture, with everything lying there, on the bottom. Frustrating. Sometimes I felt that way in French, too, but I always ended up sensing the whole structure of everything, in meanings and words, inward and outward, at any level, in any dimension.

I walk along New York streets—and they are prison to me. I want desperately to be back in Europe, to touch the old stones, to be lost in the nonparallel, noncrossing streets, to find familiarity in faces, clothes, and smells. I don't like America. I hate New York. I hate my life.

~ ~ ~

With Marc, my first American friend and colleague, we speak an international language of literature, cinema, politics, philosophy. He is no different from my beloved French or Russian friends, except that he eats with his fingers and is always late. We can function at the level I am used to: quotations from French poetry, Russian jokes, Italian movie directors. It is not just the quality of the verbal form that I am obsessed with, but the contents in the form of normal intellectual sharing. So these people are everywhere, aren't they? So these things are here, too, thank G-d!

~ ~ ~

I found another freelance teaching job where I can use my French and Russian. This kind of face-to-face teaching, in a luxurious, comfortable Manhattan suite, to wealthy, motivated language students, businessmen who plan to travel abroad, artists and theater producers, is so different from my business school environment! These people have a different scope of problems and their brains are so open to learning. They don't have to care about their next day survival, about the rent, and about how to build a decent future. I feel misplaced, even though it is intellectually much more rewarding. I feel that the fantasy part of me, the one from an elegant Paris café, does not work any more. The immigrants I teach English to suddenly appear closer, and their poor Brooklyn reality is something much more tangible.

Why is Marc saying, alluding to my depression, "You must love your students," and something about reading American literature?

~ ~ ~

Hating America does not help me. It has something to do with building my life, my job search, my self search. What do I know about these people, their lives and values, their history? But I can't know now, I don't have the time, I have to survive and support my family, take care of everything and everybody.

~ ~ ~

I got one more evening teaching job, ESL. I teach basic English to elderly Russian people. The school is disgusting. There is this so familiar nauseating smell of a Soviet well-established cheating mechanism, of everybody's involved in the comedy, and me, again, like in the Soviet Union, being forced to participate. I pay taxes to the government, working day and night, so that these people can get their financial aid, stipends, books, stay on welfare, work off the books—and do me a favor by coming to class without a pen and paper. One more illusion debunked—the one of an honest society! Socialism in any form generates dishonesty!

I have interesting conversations with our apartment owner, about Anna Akhmatova, Marina Tsvetayeva, Alexander Block, my poetic translations from Russian. We talk about Russian poetry, Borges and Marquez, and he is amazed at how much we have read and learned, coming from the country of total isolation. He is very interested in Russian culture and history. He is thinking!

No wonder his apartment became our home. I do feel at home there. When I close the door behind me, with all this strange world left outside, and walk into my fortress, I am home. I never regret leaving Russia: I just want the new world to belong to me. I think about Herman Hesse's story about a man who comes to a resort to calm his nerves and has terrible neighbors who fight loudly every day. He hates them with all his heart; he spends all his time hating them deeply for their disturbance when suddenly, right before it is time for him to leave, he realizes that hating them did not advance him anywhere. So he thinks of a possibility to change his attitude if life circumstances cannot be changed. He makes himself love them and respect them as human beings and even finds a lot of charm in their behavior and personalities; he gets involved in compassion and sympathy for humankind, so that, by the end of the story, he leaves the hotel with a profound love of these people, his nerves calmed down and his soul relieved and open. He wishes he could have taken this attitude from the very beginning....

Can I try to love New York, love America, love people? Not the fantasy about people and about the country, as I did before, but the reality? It is very hard, much harder now, because it's my reality, my life, not abstract, not literary, not poetic and not just intellectual.

While learning French, I traveled into the depth of the language because I was in love with its culture and the cream of its people, but had I ever faced the real culture, real life, real people, in all their diversity and not just mirrored in literature and movies? I never had to create my real self, to find my niche in the real society, to function with love in the real world. Instead, I always sought refuge in a double or triple life, to defend myself, and to use my creativity reinventing myself. The only thing I loved was the fantasy, and I hated the real world around me. I have to learn how to love it. Then my English will touch base with real meaning.

~ ~ ~

Chapter 9

Healing

Calgary, Canada, is the city of oil business, cowboys, beer, and what remains of its fame as an Olympics place. It is the town where the weather is cool in summer, the sky is clear, the air is dry, and the trees and flowers look and smell like in Russia. Its downtown, like most U.S. middle-sized cities, is a concentration of the reflections of skyscrapers, mirroring the blue sky on a sunny day or generating blackness, seemingly coming from within, when it rains. On weekends, it is completely dead—a horrifying no-man's land, abandoned by civilization. The city's population, according to a city development project, lives in the suburban residential area, surrounding the business center, in little or big houses, with neatly manicured lawns. The city and its life is so structured and organized that the impression is terrifying: There is something super- or almost nonhuman about it.

I lived in a neat, polished, and waxed three-story apartment building with flowers inside and out, for business travelers, with nicely kept, although pretty standard, furnished suites, with little kitchens, terraces looking out at the park, and maids doing all the housework. There was nothing much to do in my spare time in Calgary but socialize, eat, drink, visit, and see the surrounding mountains and lakes. I did not drive at that time, so I had to rely completely on my students and their families, who did a great job, entertaining and touring me.

My job did not really leave me a lot of free time for entertainment because I taught Russian in 10-day modules, without breaking for weekends. I had time off only between modules. The idea was to immerse students entirely, 8 hours a day, for 10 days straight, in the language and culture. After 80 hours of this "crash course," my students, diverse by background, level of education, and profession, all employees of Gulf Canada, were sent to

Russia, directly to the oil fields, to work in a joint venture. The company hired the language school where I had been teaching Russian and French on a freelance basis, and the school director offered me the exciting contract to work in Canada for the whole summer, with all expenses paid. During that period, I taught 60 people who are now working in Russia: Many of them are very successful in their business and linguistic ventures.

The offer came at a period of my life when, after teaching intensive ESL programs in several business school, I was completely devastated by the fruitless search for a satisfying job. I ended up hating myself, my life, my family, my new country, New York. I grabbed at the opportunity to leave everything and everybody with a good excuse—making money—and with the hope of finding some new understanding of myself, my work, my interests, and America.

There is no coincidence nor simply "luck" in our life: Everything that happens is the fruit of our work, and Canada and what followed my Canadian experience in New York was a logical development, a turn, or an intersection in the geography of my life. It became a central chapter in the book of adventures I am writing, the establishment of my English-speaking U.S. identity, when the third language found its place and came to peace with the others. Yes, I needed that break from the third year of the process of survival in the United States; from the worries about my daughter, my husband, my parents, my grandparents; from the energy-draining hours of teaching in two or three schools; from the hard lessons of acculturation; from the burden of independence where I was the only one responsible for my own decisions.

At that time I did not know who I was anymore. Nobody seemed to care about my broad professionalism, erudition, and knowledge: I had to prove it, to show it, to share it—but with whom? Academia, the only place where I felt I would find these people, was absolutely deaf to my desperate calls for help and I was ready to terminate my attempts to make my dreams come true, in the transformation of the fruits of my intrinsic freedom back in Russia into the freedom of choice in America. I was tired and reluctantly ready to accept a dramatic career change: becoming a computer program-mer or studying law—just getting practical and using my potential for a better life, like immigrants usually do, when the contract to Canada was offered to me. I felt that teaching Russian, not French or English, had a special significance for me.

I was free to experiment with my teaching any way I wanted as long as the goal could be achieved: from zero Russian to conversational, survival Russian, so that the Canadian staff of drillers, managers, administrators, biologists, environmentalists, engineers, geologists, physicists, secretaries, accountants, and the project director himself—that was the scope of the diversity I had to deal with—could make themselves understood and continue their language learning on the linguistic foundation I was to build. I also decided that they had to learn the fundamentals of reading and writing, because adult language learners must have visual support for the language sounds, and especially because the new alphabet is involved. So, everything I knew about language teaching came into play: from international words, translation, grammar rules, reading rules, teaching of language patterns and word formation to songs, limericks, jokes, and children's stories.

That is where I realized that the best results come from a happy combination of all methods, approaches, and types of activities, depending on each particular group of students, their learning style, attitudes, motivation, educational background, and exposure to other languages and cultures. Throughout the years of teaching languages, I have developed that intuition toward the classroom that lets me use the right approach out of allthe approaches I know, without rejecting any of them or using one as the exception of another. This intuition is training, experience, and resilience—and that was one of the very important discoveries I made in Canada.

But the most important discovery I made there was about myself—as a teacher, a person, an immigrant, and a language learner. That discovery helped me to go back to New York, back to my problems and responsibilities with a vague sense of knowing, and it guided me until I found what I was looking for. It helped me to understand my place in this new world, to learn love, acceptance, friendship, and comfort with the language and what this language says. I moved toward meanings.

One of the components of my teaching Russian, along with the linguistic task or as a separate lesson or interaction, was what I thought inalienable from the language: Russian culture, civilization, history, geography, art, social or political issues. The difficulty of my stance of a political refugee from the Soviet Union, of someone who suffered from the regime, fought against it and was discriminated against was to present that material as objectively as I could, to find the right tone of conversation that would prepare my students for their life in the unfamiliar world, where mentality is affected by years of slavery, but where spirit is alive and indestructible. I was afraid that I would splash out hatred, offenses, and animosity filling in my old wounds, but none of that happened.

To my own surprise, I was talking to them about the Russia I loved, my favorite writers and poets, artists and cities, people's kindness and generosity. I was talking as a mother would talk about her sick baby, with pride about the baby's achievements and with bitterness and regret about its disease. This metaphor belongs to my students who learned about the grandeur and downfalls of Russian history with amazement and who thought that with such a multidimensional intellectual and emotional input, their interest in culture substantially grew—and with it, their linguistic achievements. By the end of this emotional experience, I knew that something positive, peaceful, and enriching was coming to me—not instead, but beyond—and that this truly teaching/learning experience profoundly touched my new self. This complex process of healing, taking place in me, was receiving along with giving out. It marked the birth of a balanced social and language ego, without which functioning in a new language and culture is impossible.

People I met, my students who became my friends, were the largest part of my language/culture therapy. After 8 hours of immersion, we all, teacher and students alike, felt exhausted. After class I was often invited for a beer, for dinner, or to visit a student's home. I was taken to a blues club, to a museum of dinosaurs (Alberta is famous for the fossils found there, which, by the way, is one of the signs of the presence of oil), to an Indian powwow, to a museum of buffalos, to an Indian pub, to Lake Louise, to horse races.

I took part in the famous Calgary Stampede, the festival of cowboy culture, with chuck-wagon races, wrestling, all kinds of arena fights. I enjoyed the street fair, with singing, dancing, and performing, ate free breakfast on a chuck wagon, and watched from a saloon window a lasso competition among cowboys. The restrooms in that quite popular establishment were marked "cowboys" and "cowgirls."

All this meant a tremendous amount of emotional and factual learning: about Canada, North America, people's roots and lifestyles. Everything was discussed, shared, argued about, compared with the European way. I wanted to understand why oil field drillers are in reality farmers who are working in the oil business to support their farms. I wanted to know everything about the past and present of Canadian Indians, life on reservations, and their actual situation in Canadian society. I learned a great deal about Canadian government politics and people's attitudes to it. I explored the issue of national health insurance and discovered its benefits and deficiencies. I lived the "future shock," walking from building to building without ever having to go outside, getting lost in the glass tunnels and winter gardens with lakes and swimming pools, stores and restaurants, and seeing cars speeding underneath, without a sound, like in a science fiction movie. I found out how different values of education might be, talking to people with graduate degrees about classic European literature and films they had never heard of, and surprising them, in turn, by the fact that there are still people on this planet who do not know how to drive—which equalled in their eyes to something like not knowing how to ride an elevator. I discovered the difference between the west and the east, English and French Canada, meeting Canadians from Montreal and Quebec who had moved to the west but whose mentality, culture, way of thinking, and behavior patterns were so much closer to mine. I talked with an antisemite who openly declared he hated Jews and it was interesting to discuss why, what, and whom he hated. I discovered with curiosity that Jewishness is seen differently there than in New York, and my Canadian friends had tremendous difficulties figuring me out as Russian–Jewish–French–American; that combination was simply beyond their understanding, because many of them had never left Calgary. In this wealthy and small WASP community, cosmopolitism is a concept nobody understands.

The funniest outcome was that I represented in Calgary not only the far away, almost nonexistent Europe, but the border between the United States and Canada: an American, a New Yorker. I was the symbol of the huge, the messy, the dirty, the aggressive New York, the capitol of the world, with its dangers and its opportunities.

Because they identified me with that mysterious life in the melting pot, imaginable only from television or movies, I suddenly felt that I really belonged to that life, that after years of wandering, I finally had landed in the right place, as diversified as my background of intercultural adventures and fantasies and as challenging as my intellectual interests. With the eyes of my cowboys, I saw myself as an American, a New Yorker, which translates for me as "citizen of the world": traveling, learning, moving, running, and differentiating Brooklynese from Manhattan Upper East or West Side accents. I knew I would find a spot for myself, my own niche in all that diversity, and I suddenly felt bored and misplaced in the clean, wealthy, dull environment of the town with winter gardens, shopping malls, and luxurious restaurants, where a doctor, driving a Toyota, would lose all his clients.

***

We are all social creatures. No matter how hard we try to draw on the inner sources, we still need other people to tell us who we are. With them and through them, we receive and give social information, learn about and reinvent ourselves. If this social and self-actualizing experience is at the same time a language learning experience, then the wholeness of the new identity building process—thinking, speaking, crying, joking, laughing, and dreaming, expressed in a foreign language—becomes a creative discovery.

When I flew back home, noticing in the back of my linguistic mind the difference in accents between the U.S. and the Canadian customs officials,

I had mixed feelings of loss and of gain. I cried a lot on the plane, saying good-bye to Calgary, friends, my Russian course, and the old confused me I had left behind. I smiled, looking at the gifts and postcards with greetings and good-byes in broken Russian that I received at the farewell party at Gulf Canada. Our closeness was a mutual thirst for fresh water in the beginning of our adventures; my students would go to Russia to work, learn, find new friends, and possibly create new selves; I would go back to New York—to do the same thing. Our teaching/learning joint venture left us, on both sides, filled with knowledge and mixed emotions about ourselves, people far away and near, and the smallness of the world in which we live.

Chapter 10

French Disease

It's like an illness: I'm sick with bilingualism.

—Elsa Triolet, *La Mise en Mots*

I only touched the books. I wanted to pick one, to read some of my favorite French writers, but I could not. A mysterious force kept me away: My hand pulled them one by one, and then slowly put them back on the shelf, caressing them. What am I afraid of? Is it the fear to be back or the fear not to be back? Both prospects seemed horrifying.

My French books are the only visible symbols of my French soul. That soul embraced people, passions, achievements, suffering, and love. No matter why I had to construct it—for defense, survival, or against confusion—it is still mine. The price I paid for being fully fluent in French is this sadness, the "afterlanguage," the bitter aftertaste. Not living and using the language acquired feels like losing a limb, a friend, a lover. Bilingualism is a way of life; it is an absolute involvement in two cultures and two societies that means, among other things, close ties with people—language speakers, and with the cultural heritage—these people's spirit. It is an emotional experience. When these bilingual ties are broken, there is an emotional dysbalance, a psychological discomfort, similar to nostalgia, a "language sickness."

I became aware of my sickness only after my first 2 years of immigration. As a result of unsuccessful attempts to find work with French, in the business and academic world, I transferred my fiasco to what seemed the surrogate of French life: visiting French bookstores in Manhattan, buying most expensive records of French chansonniers that we could not afford, seeking the "French ambience" in Greenwich Village and SoHo, eating croissants, and writing long confusing letters to my friends in France, something about being "a European intellectual." I was so obsessed with my French self, following my usual pattern of self-assertion, that it finally took some dangerous elitist and arrogant proportions. That was definitely not me—neither French nor Russian, nor anything else. I was alarmed. I realized I was afflicted with a disease, the French disease, something deeply abnormal, almost pathological. Something was telling me that my attitudes were wrong—especially wrong here, in America. This something was stopping me from a better adjustment: I wanted to recover, to live a healthy life.

And then it started to make sense to me. I did not have to continue being French in America. I did not have to expose my French self as a defense shield against the society. I did not have to exhibit my French identity in order not to be Russian, Jewish, Soviet. I did not have to create a fantasy of the noble, old, and beautiful French culture. I did not have to suffer from being exiled in my own country: I was not the *émigré de l'intérieur*—I was the *émigré de l'extérieur* now! My role is not seeking refuge in language learning; it is seeking a normal, healthy, and better life. I could build an American Self and a real life with it, reinventing myself with the language once again, engaging myself in a new journey, with adventures, people, interesting literature, cinema, music. However, this time I would do it for a healthy purpose—for taking the responsibility of the real life, with a real career, with real benefits for my family.

When I figured that out, new roads opened to me. It was like gaining eyesight after a period of blindness. I found interesting work. It did not have to do with French. With teaching English, I discovered more and more about American literature, I got to know interesting people, I made friends. Smiling to myself, I gradually became not only fully proficient in English, but an expert in teaching English as a second language. I assumed my American self.

It was not easy to say good-bye to my pretty self of a French *émancipée*, sitting on a terrace of a café in Paris, chatting about the last novel by Marguerite Duras or the film of Godard. That loss was painful, but at the same time it did not feel like a loss anymore.

Could I have become proficient in English as fast as that, without being fluent in French? Could I embrace and feel the depth of the culture? Would I meet so many wonderful people if I had not met and loved my French friends? Would I have been able to continue to be a linguist, a writer, a scholar, a researcher—a creator, without my French life? I did not have to separate myself; I had to reunite myself. I am not losing; I am only gaining. There is too much of myself, and there will be more and more. With each language and each identity, there will be more life, more love, and more growing. Multiplicity is the adjustment.

I am caressing my French books as my old friends. Maybe they will be silent for a while, until their richness and soul wake up in a different form, not painful and conflicting, but productive and happy. Like a new course I could design and teach. Like a seminar I could convene. Like this book.

Chapter 11

Driver's License

What keeps you going isn't some fine destination but just the road you're on, and the fact that you know how to drive.
                                                        —Barbara Kingsolver, *Animal Dreams*

I am driving to work, almost completely relaxed, enjoying every moment in the car. The car is my little home now, where I have learned how to drive and feel completely at ease. It feels as if my body has found a different dimension in space, and freedom has become a bodily concept. It is new and exciting. Those who drive all their life, as do the majority of Americans, are not aware of these feelings: driving a car in this country is not considered a luxury nor a special personal achievement, but a skill necessary for everyday commuting. To me it is a great personal success, a stake in my immigrant growing up process (my friends say, "Look at you! You are a big girl now!"), and a step up on the stairs to my American dream. I know I would always feel handicapped if I had not learned how to drive.

Back in Russia, I couldn't even imagine myself driving a car. I often had dreams about myself at the wheel—and my dreams usually turned into nightmares, ending in terrifying car accidents. For some reason, I even developed a phobia about riding in a car, which was probably an emotional transfer of other fears, suppressed by my consciousness: the feeling of insecurity as a result of my jewishness and the sense of living in the impasse.

Rare families in Moscow had their own cars, and if they did, it was considered a luxury. Women driving was associated with Brigitte Bardot movies, with that incredibly free and wealthy west, where even women drove their own cars, holding the wheel in one hand and a cigarette in the other. These stereotypical pictures fed us with illusions about the Western reality—and the more real they seemed, the more cinematographic or illusionary they became. Besides, driving in Russia was considered an exclusively male occupation (something like riding a horse), and the rare personal cars in use were always the man's domain: his baby, his home, his favorite pastime. I know some immigrant Russian couples who still cannot overcome these patriarchal ties with their past, where men do not let their wives become independent drivers (i.e., independent individuals). I believe that driving (historically equivalent to riding a horse) had a lot to do with the liberation of women in America since the time of the conquest of the West. It contributed to the idea that there are no male or female specialized know-hows and prevented sexist stereotyping.

Two years ago, in New York, it still seemed almost impossible to me: would I ever overcome my fears, acquire skills, quick reactions, automatisms? I practiced, with my husband's patient help, for almost a year, repeatedly failing my driving test. It seemed that I would never make it—it was just beyond me!

Going through this one more test of immigration, I thought about my ESL students. Are they, just like me on the road, struggling with the "crazy language," falling into despair and helplessness? Do they also feel handicapped, with their awkward English pronunciation and foreign-sounding inflexions, with the unfamiliar and tongue-twisting sounds? Does their linguistic inadequacy feel as babyish as having a driving phobia, as frustrating and hopeless as the insurmountable, almost animal desire to close the eyes, scream, and stop the car in the middle of the busy street, admitting your shameful helplessness? Are they always as tense as I was at the wheel, fearing that they will never relax, never feel comfortable, speaking or writing in English? Do their academic failures in English classes, which equal their personal failures in American life, foretell more failures ahead—just like with my driving test?

Driving, versus linguistic performance, does not involve intellect, socialization, and other mental and psychologically loaded complex operations. It consists of pure skills, trained by practice, which lead to a sense of comfort on the road, when driving itself is not an effort anymore, but a pleasurable thing to do. However, the outcomes of the training are similar: Being fluent and fully functional in the language spoken in the country feels the same as being comfortable at the wheel of the car on the road, fitting in a parking space, moving backward, and speeding on a highway. When you are comfortable at the wheel, you are free to go anywhere you want; when you function in a foreign language in all its aspects, you can live your life in a new country, with everything this life involves: work, fun, intellectual pleasures, business, emotional freedom. As a language learner, I have experienced only short periods of discomfort and frustration with my language acquisition; as a driver, this period of learning was long and horrendous. It was a revealing process, therefore, about the individual variables in human learning and an insight into the problems, struggle, and suffering of a less successful or slower language learner.

My experience of learning how to drive shows, however, that there are no insurmountable barriers in human learning, that what seems impossible in the beginning finally becomes possible, and that there are no standard ways, styles, or time frames for human learning: Individual variables are endless.

* * *

I am driving to work, almost relaxed, enjoying every moment of being in the car. It is my little home now because it takes me from one home to another, to Kingsborough College, where I am teaching. I take the same road every day: first I drive along Brighton Beach Avenue, under the subway bridge, a dirty, ugly commercial street, the "Russian paradise," where all the food sold looks like it has been cooked by my grandmother. It is also called "little Odessa," partly because it is on the ocean shore, partly for its deeply provincial, Eastern European spirit. It is mostly populated by Russian immigrants from little or middle-sized Ukrainian or Byelorussian towns similar to the ones my ancestors came from.

Maybe that is the reason I feel I have traveled back in time when I am on Brighton Beach: either in the Jewish shtettles in czarist Russia or at the period of NEP, established by Lenin in the 20s as a transitional regime between capitalism and socialism, when little private businesses were allowed and flourished until all the *nepniks* were smashed by Bolsheviks. It was a colorful and picturesque period in Russian history, generously depicted by famous Russian writers and poets—a time when there was plenty of food and revolution seemed a beautiful verbal eventuality. Russian people on Brighton Beach live in the "verbal eventuality" of America, taking advantage of the elements of American socialism (welfare, government housing, foodstamps) and making their provincial petit-bourgeois dreams come true. They constructed here the Russia of their dreams, where clothes are bright, hair is red, and the language is blended Ukrainian-Russian-English with a Yiddish accent (isn't it Orwell's "Newspeak"?). They seem happy on their little island, and I look at them as at my "genetic pool."

I have very little in common with them. I speak normative Russian or English, I consider myself belonging to America, to Europe, to the world, with different cultures, foods, and colors of skin. My students at Kingsborough, children of Brighton Beach Russians, value me for being Russian, for being on their side of the fence, and at the same time they often tell me that I am different from them: American? Cosmopolitan? European?

When we first came to the United States and landed on that Russian Jews' island, I could not believe my eyes: I had never seen these people in my whole life! They appeared more strangers than Americans, and their culture was different from mine in many ways, maybe except for food. I walked in Brighton Beach, my eyes closed—from shame, alienation, and frustration.

When I started teaching at Kingsborough, the sense of connection to my "genetic pool" transpierced me. Different, American, European, cosmopolitan, or whatever my differentness from these people was, I felt like a missionary, a mediator between them and the rest of the world. Their children, my students, do not want to be isolated on that island; they need education, Americanness, social and psychological adjustment in order to be propelled into a wider world, a wider culture. And I was there, as the best example to follow, the most reliable person to trust, the most cultured and educated role model—both in their way and in the American way.

When I drive along Brighton Beach now, I see the ugliness and the provincialism created by my compatriots: silly, naive, uneducated, and unprepared for the future. They need me in order to give their children a chance—and I drive faster to a different world, Manhattan Beach, where provincial Russia suddenly becomes provincial America, with little green streets, architecturally eclectic styles of little and big houses—a superclean, wealthy residential neighborhood that logically ends with the college gate. My way to college is a miniature road to America, for many immigrants, Russians among them, from the Old world to the New world. College will let them out, with their English and other classes completed, with their American diplomas, American clothes and behavior, from their parents' nest to the present and future, to a different geography of the New World, far from NEP and far from their parents' dreams of paradise.

Kingsborough was the first bright color in my black-and-white immigrant depressive world. The immigrant depression, I noticed, is an aesthetic disease: We are easily disgusted by foreign ugliness perhaps because one of the hopes of immigration is the hope for aesthetic harmony, one of the facets of a "better life." Brooklyn, for the most part, was not exactly eye caressing, and I still hoped for an environment where I could see beauty every day. When I arrived on the Kingsborough campus, there it was, inside and out, with ocean views and architectural consistency: the rooms, the hallways, the library, the equipment, the conveniences, and facilities for teachers and students—everything there seemed aesthetically thoughtful. I could not believe that I would see it every day and would even become part of it.

I met new people; with curiosity and admiration I listened to their conversations, participated in the department ESL meetings; real teaching and learning was going on there, with faculty and administration caring, thinking, and creating. My adjunct teaching position was a challenge to me: I had never taught academic ESL, I had never been involved in the U.S. higher education system. I had to learn fast, becoming a sponge, absorbing new speaking and behavior styles, information about college, new philosophies and teaching techniques, new books and teaching materials.

For the first time in my life I really liked my boss, the ESL program director. I was grateful that he had given me that chance to learn, that he trusted my abilities and foreign credentials, and that he was the one to realize that the college and students needed me, on that side of the fence. In my past experience, a director is a person to fear and not the one with whom to openly converse. It was easy to ask him questions or to express concerns about students, materials, assignments, tests. My boss, consciously or unconsciously, nurtured me, raised me as a new professional, and helped me to learn and discover. My classical European academic background, education, and language teaching experience was enriched by new methodologies and ideas my director and colleagues taught me; every day I worked hard to make them belong to me; every day I struggled with my conservative training; every day I questioned my own experience.

Thanks to many people at Kingsborough, I started seeing light at the end of the tunnel, found a professional commitment, a career, a goal, a profession that could combine all my professions and that could become the most rewarding of all. The social meaning of my work, responding to the vital needs of immigrants, brought me to an understanding of my new role in the new country. These people returned to me my self-confidence when it was almost lost in the battlefield of immigration, and helped me acquire the sense of standing on the earth with both feet, which led me further, to more work, studies, and creativity. My doctoral program and this book are the fruits of this transformation and are more proof of language learning as meaning-making, discussed earlier, of the positive effect of the emotional factors, and of the fluency coming from extensive reading, writing, speaking, and listening—communicating for a meaningful purpose, with real-people, in a real life situation, where learning was my salvation.

I loved my ESL students—motivated, interested, learning fast. I felt I was telling them my own story, with each new assignment, discussion, academic advisement, or reading. I was involved in the unique significance of individual immigrant lives, where my teaching could create a possible change and even a transformation like the one that had happened to me. The more I taught, the more I studied, the more interesting and engaging it became. My interest in the affective domain and the cultural dimension of language learning has grown out of my desire to communicate to my students the idea that successful acculturation, adjustment, and love for people and cultures is an important part of their English acquisition. My fascination with the idea of the interaction of identity and language acquisition was not a theoretical stance, but a commitment to my students, whose lives were important to me. My theoretical interests were rooted in my teaching practice and everyday interaction with students, language learners and immigration survivors. I respected and admired their struggle.

My teaching/learning experience had to embrace American literature and culture. Without it, I would never have fit into the academic ESL structure, nor the modern whole language teaching system, where students read whole books and wrote projects. But most importantly, I would never have fit into the world I wanted to belong to because my own adjustment, acculturation, and language ego acquisition could come only from its authentic source—culture and culture sharing. I read new books with my students, while teaching them. I tried to teach them every semester, using the materials I did not know, so every semester added new books, texts, and of course new experience. My doctorate was of great help: American English, culture, and contemporary American literature were new dimensions of my growth, as I became multilingually whole. Becoming proficient, fully functional, educated, well-read, and cultured in English and teaching it to others were two parts of the same interactive process, the process of growth that is receiving and giving.

Was it luck or the deserved compensation of my efforts? Not only did I discover a place where I could create my home, but also I acquired family members who are indispensable for a homey atmosphere. With surprise, I realized how similar the people I meet and make friends with are, no matter what language they speak or what culture they belong to. They speak the language of kindness, intellectuality, liberalism, cosmopolitanism. They talk and behave the same way my Russian, French, English friends do. They like me for who I am, they respect me and give me credit and support. Without them, my English could not be as good as it is. It has to be good enough to express my love, my friendship, and my understanding.

When my father died and during the last months of his tormented life, I received the support only real friends can give. It was the gift of their precious time, closeness, warmth, and invaluable advice. I was honored to accept it and to deserve it. I forgot what language I spoke while crying and telling them my sorrow because the only language you speak to good friends is the language of friendship, love, and compassion.

Tara, in her white Scottish sweater, was running to me, smiling, laughing, and gesticulating. I watched her approach as in a movie, with tears of joy: It was real! Her face was a century old, as if I had known her before I was born. I told myself, "This is how friends look." I had had this weird vision before: a momentum, an inexplicable déjà-vu, bumping into her in the college hallway. My father was already very sick then, and I was devastated with despair and confusion, dealing with hundreds of things at the same time. She hugged me, and I cried for the first time in my American life on the shoulder of my dear American friend, who for a moment seemed to have always existed in my life. Like my old Moscow friends, she sometimes calls me for no reason, "just touching base," or gives me an improvised visit with Italian pastry, or sends me an unreadable note via my college mailbox. I recognize then that regardless of the topics of our conversations (which she keeps defining as "dialogues"), this is the eternal, the a-linguistic, the a-cultural relationship that, among other meanings and values, brings about language and culture.

Paula said, "I want to know more about your father." Watching the sunset from the Russian restaurant on the ocean boardwalk where she took me, I did my best to tell her in English my love for my dad and what he meant in my life. It was the best thing a friend could do: make me cry, and sob, and speak, and make me feel that I am not alone here, I do have friends!

I reinvented myself in these friendships, becoming American: We laugh, make jokes, exchange news, cry on each other's shoulders and talk a lot about teaching, about our students, and books to read in class. We support each other in struggle, suffering, family tragedies. I don't have the only corner on suffering; they have it, too—each in a different way, scope, and level. These friendships helped me to move away from immigration as a micro-life aside from other lives and to realize that I am like everybody else now. I believed that my American identity in the English-speaking setting would not allow my friends to see who I really am. Marc told me, "But I have a pretty good guess!" This "guess" is what I am: the essence of a person behind languages and cultures. This essence can be seen only through the transparency of authentic human relationships.

There are other meaningful relationships with people we met in the United States. They live with me, in the same world and share everything the language can or cannot express. All of them contribute, in one way or another, to my new American identity building, to my life in contact with languages, since they interact with me socially, emotionally, linguistically. Unlike my stories about the past—the "past perfect" or the "past indefinite," when I could approximate my narrative with what really happened, my present—the "present continuous," is not the time frame to give definitions or attribute images. The narrative goes on, with the story of my life: It is being written right now, it is a continuum. The language acquisition, along with it, has no end or limits, it cannot be taught or learned by portions, parts, or skills; it is limited only by us, by the limits we set in our lives, by feeling, thinking, and creating. The urge of creating an identity in the new language and culture is the same as finding a home, with loved ones. We want to feel comfortable at home, fully functional, loving, and loved. In order to do that, we have to open our minds and hearts, be giving and receiving, and work hard. Home is not easy to find.

* * *

I am driving home, almost relaxed, enjoying every moment in the car. I finally got my driver's license, as a result of hard work, patience, and struggle with myself and others. It was a must to have this driver's license in order to be on the road, across the continents and countries, make some tough turns, and keep myself driving, no matter what, with the panoramic view behind and ahead, and my own image blurred in the mirror.

Chapter 12

Frank or Pete?

Frank was a big blond guy in his late 40s. At the time that I met him, he looked like a typical American to me: there was something in him that reminded me of the baseball games that were shown on Soviet television. Many Russians saw Americans that way because it was the only image available. After all, we create stereotypes out of the information we have. For that reason, I noticed later how those images were failing with more information appearing. Russian immigrants often express their surprise meeting a nontypical American: "You don't look American to me!" WASP was the only image created in the isolation of Soviet life, therefore, Russians always found that the typical American is a bit like a Siberian: He comes from the land with a lot of space, and his culture is eclectic, as opposed to the European one.

Frank wore a windbreaker winter jacket that none of us had seen before and constantly took pictures with his tiny camera, a miracle of Japanese technology. He was referred to us by other Americans who had visited Russia and who, in their turn, knew our American relatives. Frank, knowledgeable about the KGB, the way people are from the American television movies and mystery books, called my aunt from a phone booth, for the "walls had ears"; he did not want "them" to trace the call and involve everybody in trouble. She immediately invited him to her place. We had a charming evening together and found out that Frank decided to visit Russia because of his love of classical music, particularly Russian opera composers. That fact was particularly amazing because Frank, as far as we understood, did not belong to any "intellectual profession."

I clearly remember giving Frank a tour around Moscow and telling him the stories about Moscow architecture like this one. Hotel Moscow on

October 25 Square (now its name is probably back to the old, familiar to every Muscovite, *Manezhnaya*), built under Stalin, has two absolutely asymmetrical wings. Stalinist architecture, monumental, oppressive, imperious, could not have been designed this way on purpose. The legend of its construction says that when two final projects were submitted for Stalin's choice and approval, he, the expert in linguistics, genetics and other bourgeois sciences, signed both, either by negligence or inadvertence. The architects in charge of the ideologically most important project, were so horrified by the prospect of going back to Stalin to clarify the matter (it could have cost them their lives) that the only plausible decision they made was to build the hotel with both designs. Therefore, as a monument to the greatest human fear which engenders the ridicule, the building on Manezhnaya, near the Red Square, has two totally different in structure and design, asymmetrical wings.

Stories about what Moscow is really about, what is going on, and what people's lives look like transformed Frank's visit of a regular American tourist to an intellectual and spiritual quest. He told me later that without us, he would have never been able to learn the truth, to embrace the complex Soviet reality, and, most importantly, attribute to the country a "human face."

Frank's visit was perhaps the first encounter I had with the American culture, language, and reality. Frank was a nice, pleasant, and grateful guest, and I felt quite comfortable with him, despite my poor, unpracticed English. I discovered, talking to him, that my language represents only sets of rules I had learned in class, and that it had no spirit and no soul. It was a distant shapeless cloud suspended in the sky quite artificially, and therefore it did not produce real communication, which is in its major part emotional—there was no rain coming from that cloud.

Frank did not try to correspond with us because he felt it could jeopardize our already jeopardized enough lives. But a few years later, we heard his voice again, from a Moscow phone booth. He had enjoyed his first visit so much that he made up his mind to come again. He confessed that he had been missing us and that this time he came to see us, not Moscow. And again, there were long walks along Moscow streets and endless conversations about politics and the world at the big and full of food Russian tables, which were set by some kind of incomprehensible magic, out of empty shelves in the stores. The secret of this plentiful hospitality was in two most important rules every Soviet family followed: first, the storage, and second, the ingenuity. We all used to have cupboards, closets, and freezers full of canned and frozen foods. And we all knew how to cook, bake, and create something out of nothing: the exotic recipes were born out of shortage and poverty, and refined tastes amazed those who are used to consume ready-to-eat foods from a supermarket. Frank was delighted by the meals he ate at our homes, by the sincerity and openness of his Soviet friends, by the atmosphere of holiday created around his visit.

My friendship with Frank involved me in two interesting journeys: one was his personality and view of the world, and the other was the American culture he had brought to me. Its meaning fully unfolded to me when I saw the America of his home and learned to differentiate different Americas and different dreams. When Frank told us about his life in Vermont or his childhood in Massachussets, his stories, half understood not only because of the imperfections of our language, but mostly because of the vague awareness of the culture, seemed deprived of the meaning. I have no recollection at all of his personal accounts: he came to us from nowhere and could hardly be existent. We saw the real Frank only in the context of our lives, Moscow streets, or his favorite music. Our relationship was similar to the ones people see in their dreams; there was a sensation, an impulse, a flash of colors and sounds. As we remember our dreams, we remembered Frank, who had appeared twice from nowhere and where he had disappeared. The international airport, which smelled of the foreign flavors and fragrances (that is what the "nowhere" smells like!), was the only material exit, the black hole, where my friends vanished. Frank went there, too.

Our eventual immigration to America, which suddenly became real, did not bring about any connection with Frank, our pleasant guest to Moscow, a ghost from an unknown land. In the turmoil of packing and good-byes, during the hardships of the transition in Italy, and finally, in New York, I forgot all about him. But once, sitting on the bed, the only piece of furniture in our first home on Brighton Beach, and staring at the white blank wall in the white blank prostration, I managed somehow to associate Frank, the happy, healthy, radiant person from nobody-knows-where, with the grey Brooklyn landscape, brown bricks, and a voice on television news, which had a similar inflection. Without any hope nor real expectations, I dropped a postcard to him, and when I was writing his address, with the post office box number, I felt exactly like this poor orphan boy from the Chekhovian story, who addressed his letter, begging his grandfather to take him back home, "to the village, my grandfather."

In the busy and short, seemingly meaningless first days and weeks of our struggle to survive in America, I forgot all about it, until one day I answered the door, and a big beautiful, green plant in a nice basket was handed over to me. In amazement and incredulity, I murmured something about this being the wrong address. But the delivery boy checked the address and the name: It was positively for me. I opened the tiny white envelope attached to the plant. The card, with an unfamiliar handwriting on it, said, "Welcome to America! Frank." It seemed to me that I had seen that plant before, in my other life. It is like the reverse story of Sigmund Freud's dream whose meaning lay in the identification of a plant he was unable to recognize. Freud finally recalled that he had seen it in one of his fellow students' house back in his childhood years. The analysis of the dream unfolds from there. I felt that this plant, vice versa, brings me back to my dream of an American guy, Frank, who loved Russian music, Russian culture, and us, his Russian friends. I put the plant on the floor. I turned it around. I watered it. And I said aloud in English, "Welcome to America."

Frank's plant is alive and has been living with us for all the years in New York.

Soon after this, Frank called us. He said that he had planned for the three of us, my husband, my daughter, and me, to go visit him in Vermont. He said that he would drive to New York to take us to his place. He said that he remembered and loved us. We were delighted.

Our trip to Vermont was the beginning of my discovery of America. It was also the door out of my immigration depression, and the best confirmation for a common saying among Russian immigrants: Brighton Beach is not Brooklyn; Brooklyn is not New York; New York is not America. We drove in Connecticut (strangely and unrecognizably pronounced as "Conneticut"), Massachussets, New Hampshire (I wanted to pronounce it "Hampshaer," the British way), and Vermont. We saw the clean little towns, the woods, the churches; we heard a different accent, and we discovered different attitudes and a different culture.

My husband spoke some broken English he learned during his career as a delivery boy, and my 5-year-old daughter had just started preschool and, to our greatest surprise, began uttering whole English sentences. I was the main interpreter, the only real speaker in the family during the conversations with Frank, his wife, and other people we met at their house. This role overwhelmed me because I did not feel that it was okay anymore to have such a poor command of English in the English-speaking country as opposed to my performance back in Moscow. I suppose that is how the difference between a foreign and a second language feels like. I am always hard on myself as far as the language performance is concerned. Is it because I consider myself a linguist in all the aspects of this word's semantics?

Frank's life, in a small cabin in the woods, with nobody around but skunks and birds, was such a difference from our first home in Brooklyn! In Russia, this lifestyle would be associated with complete wilderness, but here the level of civilization was the same as in the city. The car drove him everywhere he wanted, including various stores and restaurants; his house was equipped with the same things every city person would have; his intellectual interests were satisfied through university libraries and bookstores, museums and concert halls in the nearby towns. That was beyond my understanding, and it took me years to get used to the idea that civilization and culture are two separate concepts and they should not be confused. In Europe, we have stereotypes about "the woods," the cities, and people's social and intellectual status. The American history, however, is constructed on the non-European type of democracy and is reversing many stereotypes. For instance this one: Where do Americans get mushrooms? Of course in the supermarket! The Russians associate the mushrooms with wild woods!

We were happy to pick huge, never-gathered mushrooms in Frank's woods (another discovery was that most of the woods belong to somebody and that we could not walk there without this person's permission). We carefully cleaned and cooked the mushrooms, which deliciously smelled from the soup and the stew, but our friends did not seem to be eager to eat them. For them, *real* mushrooms, with the unique smell of the forest, the soil, and the rain, could be dangerous to eat. In vain, we explained that every Russian, from the early childhood, is taught how to tell a bad from a good mushroom, and is well experienced in this historically connotated enterprise. Had Americans ever felt hunger? Had Americans ever gone to the woods to get food?

The intercultural gaps are so difficult to fill: Our whole persona seems to resist this learning by suppressing the rational, the analysis, and the reflections.

Frank was the first human soul in the new world who cared about us, and I suddenly stopped seeing him the way I had done in Moscow. He appeared as a down-to-earth, pragmatic American, with a real wife, real problems with his children, and some real ideas about where his country was going. Now our roles were reversed, like everything in this story, by the American context. His change, or the change of my perception of him, was so dramatic that by the second day I realized that even his name was different. Was I hallucinating? But no: Everybody called him Pete.

It turned out that "Frank" was his "official" name that he never liked. Since his childhood he adopted a nickname: Pete. When he traveled to Russia he felt that he had to introduce himself with his "official" name, the one on his passport, because in the country of spies and informers, his double identity could be misinterpreted. Why he introduced himself as Frank to us, not the Soviet officials, is still a mystery to me. Perhaps it reflects the vague, unconscious fears generated by cultural stereotypes or false assumptions that people make in the new country. I felt that my understanding of America and of Frank/Pete was subject to the same fears, false assumptions, and confusion.

During several days with Frank we discovered a country and a lifestyle seemingly incompatible with what we thought was America back in Brooklyn. I cried bitterly when we got back "home." I wanted to go to America.

Frank, who hated New York and was a strong proponent of a quiet country life, started feverishly helping me get a job in Vermont. As do many people in the role of parents or guardians—and Frank definitely assumed that role with us—he transferred his life, his world view, and his values to others. It is always hard to figure out that our life, built with specific personal circumstances and background, might not or cannot be the same for these loved others. Frank went to the libraries and universities, made phone calls, and did research on what might be a good job for me in his whereabouts. He sent me the information he had found indicating the amount of miles from that place to his house. Because the miles did not tell me anything, I kept asking him about "minutes." We seemed to be speaking different languages.

My job search was a failure, and Frank could not help me get oriented in the academic field. My still poor command of English, my insufficient knowledge of the American culture, and imperfect writing skills were tangible barriers in the process. However, I still hoped that our relocation to Vermont (because it is so green and beautiful), closer to Frank is the solution to our immigration problems. Very often, culture shock makes people feel that the physical relocation will put an end to their suffering, that there is a place somewhere on earth where life is more pleasant, where the America of their dreams really exists. At that moment it is hard to understand that the problem is inside, not outside, and that Frank is in fact Pete. I was learning the truth bitterly and gradually, going on with my life in New York, teaching, taking care of my parents and my daughter, and struggling the crisis in my relationship with my husband. Geography was irrelevant.

Frank took us all once again to his place, and then once more on a trip to Washington DC and Virginia. He and his wife were very generous and very kind to us and did their best to be as helpful as they could. They did help us, with their warmth and hospitality, so after our last trip, I came back home, not "home," and did not feel anymore that America was in Vermont. I was even ready to defend to Frank the charms of New York. By that time I learned so much about this country and its people that I conceptualized the American "escapism"—which was later confirmed by many more examples. Indeed it was quite a discovery and could not fit my earlier formed stereotypes.

Time flew with busy schedules and efforts pursuing the American dream. At some point I realized that Frank gradually stopped keeping in touch. I made every effort not to lose him by sending letters, post cards, and calling. He invariably responded by polite invitations to visit "any time," which was indeed a vague get-together project. Once, when I was in the doctoral program, I had a meeting in New Hampshire. Frank came to see me. He was, as usual, full of optimism and joy, and happy for our achievements. Our roles changed again: I was not somebody to teach or to protect and I had much less to do with Russian composers. With him I noticed the transformation of my language, my whole self, my world. We had a great afternoon in one of these townlike shopping malls that Frank had made me discover a few years earlier. I did not feel anything special about being there; I do not cook; I do not pick mushrooms. However, I do give tours around Brooklyn or New York to friends or friends of the friends who come to America from Russia. "Welcome to America!"

Chapter 13

Interculture

There is a watch repairman on Brighton Beach who used to be my student. I go to him once in a while when the chain on my watch bracelet slips off its hook. Every time that happens I remember my dad, a real handyman, who used to fix all the broken things—big and little—including electricity, for the entire family. Once he was gone, my household became Americanized; instead of fixing things, we started to throw them away. But the ritual of having this watch bracelet fixed in the tiny watch repair booth, squeezed in the entrance of the Russian bakery, is somehow important for me. So, I sigh—and reluctantly go.

My former ESL student, the watch repairman, is a soft-spoken man. When he sees me, he greets me and smiles because he knows what has brought me to him. Then he quickly hooks the end of the loose chain to the bracelet without charging me a cent. I look around—and suddenly I picture my dad walking with his cane on Brighton Beach. He is heading to the school bus stop where he picks up my daughter. His figure looks completely misplaced and ghostly among the filthy grocery stores with labels and signs in incorrect Russian and incorrect English, the nonmatching women's clothes, and the subway train passing by above his head. My father, who taught my daughter how to read and write in Russian, who listened to the Russian radio and read Russian newspapers in his New York apartment. My father who had fought in World War II when he was 17 and was among the first Soviet soldiers to take over the Reichstag. My father who recited to me Lermontov and Beranger and taught me to swim and ski. Putting the watch on my wrist, I feel I am hooked to the Russian community my father had embraced.

My vision of him is of a world entirely opposite to the one I see around me in Brighton Beach, this strange isolated land in between cultures. But I know this was his world, too. And now I have to make meaning of it.

This spring, on May 9, Victory Day, an official holiday in Russia and a personal holiday for every Russian family, I saw a group of Russian World War II veterans marching in Brighton Beach. Dressed up and wearing twinkling war medals, these 70- and 80-year-old men were proudly trying to transfer their feelings, their history, and their culture to the New World. The picture of these formerly triumphant victors was so pathetic that I could not help crying. My father once told me that there has been a continuous and fruitless struggle of the Association of the Russian War Veterans to become part of the Veterans of Foreign Wars Association. How symbolic! "Hadn't we liberated Europe from fascism together with the Americans? Why don't they want to accept us or at least show their recognition?" he would ask bitterly. Only the island of Russian culture on Brighton Beach, the Russian community, could recognize, make meaning of, and gratify these feelings.

I live close to Brighton Beach, unlike many Russian-speaking profession-als who seek job opportunities elsewhere and typically move to New Jersey or out of New York to make their American dream of their own house, two cars, and a new baby come true. I feel weird and misplaced in this refuge for new immigrants and some elderly Americans who have survived the "Russian invasion." When I meet my Russian students in the stores or in the street, they always seem surprised to see me there. Their reaction tells me more than I can tell myself: Yes, I am here physically, but I am not here socially, psychologically, culturally.

We all want to belong to "the right crowd," the environment where we fit culturally, socially, and intellectually, the subculture that goes beyond the ethnic frames. In the United States this belonging is defined by the social milieu; the milieu is defined by the community; the community is defined by the place of residence. When immigrants arrive in the United States, they, like the very first Pilgrims, literally "land" in the place with no reference to their subculture and social milieu of origin. Most likely they would find themselves in their ethnic community, where the difficulties of adjustment to their new life could be facilitated by the speakers of the same language and where they would find the security of their ethnic traditions and rituals. With time, younger and more energetic immigrants start to seek the environment that would correspond to their subculture of origin, beyond purely ethnically defined limitations. Their careers, values, political views, and intellectual interests guide them in their search for psychological comfort among others.

When we came to America, we "landed" on Brighton Beach primarily because my parents seemed to be adjusting to their new life better among their friends and family who live in the area. Because we lived and still are living a close and interdependent family life, Brighton Beach appeared to be the right common place for all of us. The convenience of being able to help each other, of being within the walking distance, and having my main teaching job only minutes away by car from my home were undeniable priorities. With time, I and my husband have found the milieu we fit into: Our friends are middle-class people, liberal intellectuals, mostly teachers, and we feel very comfortable in that subcultural niche. However, theoretically, we would be expected to live in Park Slope, the place in Brooklyn mostly populated by "our type." Thus, Brighton Beach, with its provincial Russian Jewish spirit feels like the ancestral beginning instead of representing our future aspirations. In my jump from the Soviet subculture to the American subculture, geography and ethnicity are irrelevant.

We enjoy shopping for food on Brighton Beach. It is convenient, inexpensive, and mostly good. Besides these obvious advantages, every shopping trip becomes an intellectual adventure into interdisciplinarity: cultural anthropology, history, sociolinguistics, ethnography. Comic or dramatic, the scenes I observe or participate in help me make sense of the Russian dream in America.

* * *

Invariably, I have the endless dialogue with the saleswomen in the Russian stores: "A pound of cheese please. FUNT!" (the equivalent of "pound" in Russian). She says, in Russian, "POUNT?" I reply, "Yes, FUNT!" ... this goes on forever. The salespeople don't speak Russian!

But do they speak English? Sometimes I help some of the few remaining elderly American women to shop in Russian grocery stores. I translate their requests and questions and I always hear their complaints—not about these people not speaking any English in America, but about themselves, children of Ellis Island, not speaking any Russian. They seem to feel like foreigners in this "Russian land."

Sometimes I hesitate about what language to speak, so I choose English, just in case: What a silly mistake! Who speaks English in Brighton Beach? However, I have to continue the game and even try to "act American," displaying a big smile on my face and exchanging meaningless jokes. I feel awkward and sad, trapped in the artificiality and hypocrisy. The salespeople don't understand my jokes and do take me for an American all right. But sometimes, when I am not too far into the game, I quickly switch to Russian.

For some reason I feel this game is humiliating for the person I speak to, who usually sighs with relief and gives me a grateful glance.

Once in a Russian restaurant I heard a waiter, showing American guests to their table, yell in Russian with disbelief and almost animal fear, "Foreigners! Foreigners are coming!"

And once in the neighborhood supermarket, where among Russian-speaking cashiers there are also some "foreigners," I witnessed how an elderly Russian woman was loudly screaming, trying to get her message across to a cashier, "I am telling you: This item is on sale, you charged too much for it!" The bemused cashier was staring at the woman. In vain she was trying to persuade her that she did not speak any Russian and consequently she did not understand what the woman was saying. The old lady just kept saying, slower and louder, as if she was talking to someone deaf, "Don't you understand Russian? This item is on sale!" People in the line became impatient and did their best to persuade the lady that the cashier didn't speak Russian. The woman froze. That was simply beyond her comprehension.

I think of the etymology of the Russian word for "German" (*Niemets*)—which comes from "mute." When the first foreigners appeared in Russia during Peter the Great's *perestroika*, the Russians, who had never seen foreigners in their life, thought of them as mute because they didn't understand their language. Allegedly, the history of the word Barbarian derives from a similar paradoxical phenomenon: those visitors to Greece who could not utter Greek words—Brr...Brr....

Is this world the approximation of the Soviet Empire or of what it could be under capitalism? Is this a parallel dimension of America (in Russia) or of Russia (in America) trapped in between the galaxies?

Brighton Beach represents just one type of the Russian community's social and cultural stratification. There are other milieus and layers, where, I have noticed, the intercultural and interlinguistic phenomena represent the confusion, at a different level and in a different scope.

My very energetic Russian friends, a young couple from Moscow, have started their own multimedia business on the Internet: a "virtual" greeting card store where they produce and sell animated greeting cards to buyers all over the world. Their business is a business of the future, and probably they will eventually become very rich. Their work not only requires fluency in English, colloquial and business styles, but even more important, "fluency" in the American mainstream culture and some of its subcultures: corporate, pop, entertainment, "cyber." It would seem that the Internet market and its demands, the necessity of collaboration with the field experts and of handling communication and correspondence sometimes using the professional jargon, would engage this type of business people in the endless labyrinths of contemporary culture. This has not happened to my friends who, in their own words, often feel like "a bunch of Chechens" on a subversive mission. Operating in a system of their own and denying them-selves access to a wider American culture, they have created defense shields around their fragile egos, where the virtual American reality, like the Internet, is safer than the real one. Their fear of facing the world and their own place in it is generated by the complex struggle that some of the Russian intellectuals are going through in the United States, forced to change their careers and lose their former social and spiritual identity. Young, active, successful, creative, these people move too slowly along the intercultural axis, choking in cynicism or falling into depression. The room inside the world in between the worlds becomes stuffy after a while.

At the Washington Cemetery in Brooklyn, where my father is buried, there is a big sign in Russian, "Please be advised that fresh flowers will be removed from the graves." Historically, the cemetery is Jewish, and the Jewish laws forbid flowers on the graves. Instead of flowers, a special prayer has to be said, and a visitor might want to leave a pebble as a sign of his or her presence. Russian Jews, who had lived in a Christian society that oppressed Jewish traditions, keep bringing fresh flowers to the cemetery. And even though here in the United States they are free to be Jewish, and some of them are happy to be so, they stubbornly continue to be "Russian" in their attitude to the dead. Despite the constant struggle with the cemetery administration, the removed flowers are quickly replaced, and the "Russian row" looks so colorful and so fresh in the grayish American Jewish grief. Some of my father's friends asked me if they should or should not bring the flowers in—such a typical intercultural hesitation!—and I suggested that they do the way they feel. After all, cultural rituals are created for the purposes of self-expression and relief: By belonging to them we receive support from the invisible crowd, we escape real loneliness and fear of death, we put the thinking about the unthinkable on some concrete, culturally defined tracks. And so, the intercultural confusion accomplishes here a therapeutic function.

I vaguely feel, I unconsciously know, I have gone through all of this immigrant-Russian-Jewish transition at some point of my life in the United States, which is not purely Russian culture.

After some reflection, I realize that even the foods in such abundance on Brighton Beach are not typically "Russian," nor are they merely a mixture of Eastern European, Southern European, or Western European foods. They are what these people think is Russian, Russian in America, the Russian Heaven, the Dream. These foods and the eclectic traditions—the mix and confusion of what is Ukrainian, Jewish, Russian, Polish, Armenian, Uzbek in some abstract collective understanding of being uprooted and extirpated from the land and the sky of their country—are represented on the American soil by the strange blend of the imaginary Russian and the imaginary American. (An interesting indication of this confusion is an advertisement for "Russian-French cuisine" on one of the Russian restaurants in Brighton Beach. When asked what exactly it means and what in the menu is French, the folks there were not quite sure.) And so, while taking in the American culture and language in various degrees, the Russian community is constructing some surrogate Russian culture out of what was lost or forgotten in the wars and revolutions, out of the painful past and the beautiful dream of the future far from where they were born.

In a wider sense than just a geographical denominator, Brighton Beach is a sociocultural concept, among other things represented by the Russian media: Russian radio, television, newspapers, magazines, all of the extreme rightist orientation. But besides and beyond their political views, people who claim to provide "Russian culture" to the community are also functioning in the frames of this Russian dream here in the United States. The destinies of people who were offended by the Soviet regime or just not talented enough to scale the peaks of the Soviet artistic elite are influencing the selection of media and their interpretation. Acting as ideologists, they often feed the community with an image of Russia filtered through Brighton Beach. How close or how far is it from the playful spirit of Pushkin? The existentialism of Dostoyevsky? The genius boredom of Chekhov? The cinematographic poetry of Tarkovski? The panoramic sociology of Tolstoy? From that enormous layer of human suffering converted into esthetics by Russian artists, writers, and thinkers who had conquered minds all over the world?

The world of Russian business in the United States is also an expression of American capitalism à-la-Russe. Deception, poor quality of products, and service with a touch of nostalgic Soviet rudeness and disrespect to clients, are often part, and the visible part, of Russian community life in America. When my friends and I go "for grams" (vodka is dispensed by grams in the Russian restaurants), we often make fun, in a very benign way, of what Russians consider to be acceptable service.

It took me years to realize that this strange and rich world of Russia in America had been mine, too. At some point in my acculturation I had joined that world, together with other immigrants and language learners, but I am not there anymore. I grew out of it, cognitively, linguistically, culturally. My connection to the Russian community has nothing to do with my connection to Russian culture. It is of learning, of having learned.

I am thinking about the typical errors many learners make at different levels of their English proficiency, for example, "*I am agree with the author's opinion.*" In the light of modern language acquisition research, *I am agree* may mean that the student is experimenting with the language, trying to build parallel structures (*I am happy* and *I am agree*) and needs more linguistic input to create a correct rule. Sometimes, despite numerous corrections, the error becomes fossilized and is "glued" in the learner's mind forever. One of the reasons for that might be the psychological and social distance between the learner and the language community. Sticking with the error might seem a more secure position in the learner's confrontation with the linguistic reality.

The term *interlanguage*, the hypothetical intermediate language constructed by second language learners in the process of testing hypotheses and creating language rules, a transitional system between the native and the target languages, is an attempt to explain what happens during the process of language learning. So, *I am agree* is a sign of a stage in the learning process, a "window" into the learner's mind. Experienced language teachers can identify the interlanguage stages and foster a more effective, faster movement along the interlanguage continuum.

Paralleling interlanguage, *interculture* is a surrogate world, the transitional place that makes recent immigrants' life in the United States somewhat bearable, manageable, safe. It is creatively constructed by the members of the community who are moving along the continuum in the direction of American culture in the process of learning, adjustment, and acculturation. As in the interlanguage stages, the individual variations in this movement make it far from being uniform: some speed through it (children, young and motivated people, flexible and open-minded individuals); some get stuck at various points or freeze at the beginning forever. Interculture can be useful and good for older people and new arrivals: it is being reinvented and recreated, in their minds and on the streets, in the stores and along the pages of the press. After a while in stagnation, however, interculture can become fossilized. And so, one remains on Brighton Beach forever, on an island inhabited by ghosts from the past, in the frozen lethargy, in a strange nonexistent world, a product of collective imagination.

* * *

On a different level, American culture in itself is a kind of interculture. It is a blend of various ethnic cultures modified by the American dream, of people's representations and hypotheses about their cultures in America, a transitional mode in the move forward on the intercultural continuum, where the authentic, the native, the original is being gradually forgotten and where the new, the invented, the unknown is being created. And as one of the smallest particles in this movement, partly creator and partly created, I wish I knew where I am going.

Chapter 14

Russian as a Second Language

> ... the child may attempt to blend in and be like his or her peers; the child
> may assimilate and act as if the past never existed, denying his or her cultural
> self. If he or she can be helped by teachers to embrace both worlds, an
> integrated sense of self can develop and the child can make strides forward.
> If there is no intervention, either by teachers, other adults, or peers, the child
> may feel hopelessly shut off from his past and /or become stuck at that level.
> This stage is crucial; the child can either be guided to integrate his or her
> cultural self or be left alone to discard it, only to try to regain it in later life.
> —Cristina Igoa, The Inner World of the Immigrant Child

*This story, which describes the process of my writing it, also describes the
transformational processes that occurred in me while I was writing. The discovery
that I have made here goes beyond the topic of bilingualism, but includes it, and
I hope it will make me a new person and a new mother. The underlying realities
of this story are the accumulated effects of some valuable friendships and readings:
in the process, there was "an impulse, an awareness, a goal and a will, a triggering
event, and then—realignment" (Munaker, 1996). There was the GREAT
AHA!—and the vicious circle of my mother's projection on me of what her mother
had projected on her has been broken.*

* * *

It was drizzling outside, and New York's dominant color was gray, except for
the multicolored umbrellas people were opening and closing, uncertain
about the almost invisible rain that seemed to be over and yet wasn't.

I was heading to a café in the Village where I had a rendezvous with my editor and one of the reviewers, to talk about the final changes to the last draft of my book. I was ready to let it go; I had other projects in mind; I felt burnt out and tired. However, somewhere deep in my heart, I was opening and closing the umbrella. I was ready to put a fat black period at the last word of my stories, where the truth about the multilingual self refers to my past (close the umbrella!). However, I did not feel comfortable with the idea of the past perfect (open the umbrella!). My book is about discoveries. And discoveries are happening right now, invisible like this drizzle. There is something missing in that present perfect continuous mode of my existence, which is so beautifully grasped by English grammar, the tense that many second language learners have so much trouble with. Is that because they, like me, are trying to hide the truth from themselves?

The final reviews of my book, especially one of them, reached me right into the heart, asking the questions that I had been asking myself all along. The "painful topic" the reviewer alluded to is the issue of the present and of the future: the immigrant children, my bilingual children, what is their life in connection to ours? How can I see myself, in the consistency of my life continuum, not only as a multilingual and multicultural individual and language teacher and researcher, but simply as a parent, a mother of children growing up bilingual in a twofold world?

My little daughter, Julia (*Yulia* in Russian), is 14 months old now. She has just started walking and talking. Her baby language is a derivative of Russian: This is the only language she hears from her parents, her grandmother, and her babysitter. I am enjoying watching her form her first words: trying out the plural; not understanding the negation; expressing herself with nouns. As a linguist, I am fascinated by the way she is creating her language and experimenting with it. As a mother, I am filled with joy to know her first language is Russian. As a second language and culture researcher, I know that her first language will eventually shift giving its place to English. I am already wondering how she perceives Sesame Street every morning and how she differentiates the tone, the inflexions, and the whole different world of the American reality in her sister's English—not the meaning, not yet, oh please! I know, some day she will have to go to day care or to school; she will take in the language from her peers and from the street; she will enjoy television—and that will become her life and part of who she is. And that means, we will lose her the way we know her: What a terrible idea for any parent!

I am recalling a bitter complaint, almost a moan, of my older daughter's drama club teacher, a former Russian theater director, who thought of his work with American Russian children as the biggest failure in his life, "They are not *our* children!" Of course they are not. And that is the point.

My older daughter, Pauline, now is 12, and she is going through a difficult period of adjustment as a teenager growing into adulthood. Her bilingualism only adds to the confusion of the world perception, of wanting so badly to be like everybody else, her differentness being her a priori given. She was almost 5 when we came to this country. She did not know how to read and write in Russian. She learned English within 3 months, when she went to her first American school, where the kindness of her teacher was the only special help with her ESLness. Her Russian now is better than of many of her Russian friends, even though she may occasionally make a grammar or a syntactical error. She is unwilling to read and to write in Russian, and her vocabulary is limited. But, most importantly, she does not want to learn more and she is resistant to be involved in any Russian culture-geared activities. When she is angry or upset, she throws her English to our face as her only defense shield. Nevertheless, with all her American-like behavior, she is still my child. I desperately need her to be, to remain my child. And thus—this story.

Why are so many immigrant parents worried about their children Americanizing too fast, becoming deaf to the "home language" and culture? Besides the understandable pragmatic desire to raise our children enriched by the knowledge of two languages, there is some more dramatic meaning to our anxiety. Watching my daughter growing up *American*, whatever that term means, is somewhat disturbing, painful, and confusing.

I sat down and started writing. By the end of a few weeks I realized that I had numerous pieces that did not fit together and with which I was unhappy. I was writing about the beauty of bilingualism, my father teaching my daughter to read and write in Russian and her mysterious unwillingness to do it. There was no link between my ideas and my observations. There was no truth and no discovery. I also asked Pauline, my daughter, to write about her bilingual experiences, but her writing was equally confusing. After a great deal of struggling, I left a distress call message on my editor's answering machine and decided to "sleep on" the issue during the week of my summer vacation, the one I needed and could not afford for years.

The only vacation I had was my doctoral program that required some out-of-town seminars, which were fun and full of interesting people—but still, they were not real vacation. By the end of my doctoral program, there was a long sickness of my father, who died while I was heavily engulfed in the dissertation writing. There was teaching in two or even three jobs and the frustrating full-time substitute line at my college eliminated by the magic stick of the budget crunch. Then there was pregnancy; the baby; the job search, and my 12-year-old daughter becoming an American teenager. Preparing the book for publication under these circumstances was not an easy task. Vacation! I needed real vacation!

I also wanted to take my older daughter away from her little sister and the noise of the house where the baby is always the center; to spend some quality time with her, to communicate in the silence of the nature, and finally to be there for her, just for her. We booked a cottage in Cape Cod, with a friend of mine who took her 14-year-old son. We had planned that fun trip for years over the phone and it seemed such an important accomplishment to finally make it happen.

My friend's son, Andrei, is a quiet, intelligent boy, who loves clam chowder, pancakes, and poker. I am sure he is passionate about other things, too, but on that trip he seemed reserved, locked in his own world, and—unsafe. All children experience insecurity at a certain degree, but immigrant children are more insecure than others. In the desperate attempt to keep the native language alive, in my friends' house it is forbidden to say even one English word. Doesn't this seem like a plausible solution to the problem of language and culture attrition?

I remember how silly I felt in their house facing the dilemma of finding Russian words for certain nonexistent cultural realities and concepts. Let's say there is an equivalent in Russian to the word *highway* , but it is simply not at all what a highway really is—it is just a road. And even if one can find the exact equivalent, the word might be an archaism, no longer used in modern Russian; it might have taken on a different emotional connotation or need a long paraphrase because the equivalent does not exist. And how about the spontaneous stories, jokes, rhymes which create (or are created by) the whole different culture in school or at work or in the street? Not only did I feel silly and awkward, tormenting my mind to translate the untranslatable, but I also felt humiliated by the situation of someone's having control over my language, over me. Being a determined partisan of the importance of keeping the native language and of true bilingualism, I felt in contradiction with myself.

As a rule, we speak Russian at home. I know my daughter would sense the awkwardness and the wrongness if I spoke English to her. I only do it in the presence of her or my English-speaking friends, out of mere politeness. When she was in summer sleep away camp, I faced the dilemma of printing to her some very simplistic messages in Russian or of writing to her in English. I did both, and she recognized both: These two voices are part of me and part of our relationship. Pauline (who adopted an American name, Paula, despite my attempts to explain that Pauline is a French, not a Russian name) is proud of my good English when I talk to people in front of her and especially when I talk to her teachers. I always try to suppress my discontent about her speaking English at home in certain situations, like passionate recollections of her experiences at school, or about code-switching if there is no cultural equivalent in Russian. In all my good faith in bilingualism, I have to believe in my natural instincts. It is imperative for Pauline, a definite extrovert, to seek a place in the peer group. Part of the search is to see herself through the eyes of other girls and boys, who seem to be or are self-asserted Americans. Being or feeling American (like "everybody else"—her motto of the day) brings her security and stability.

Needless to say, my daughter did not get along with the introvert Russian-speaking Andrei, who insistently spoke Russian to his mother, me, and my daughter. He even spoke Russian to his mother in the presence of other Americans. It appeared a secret language in his secure world, where he could find a nest for their close relationship. Instead of being happy about our children's communication in Russian, the Russian world suddenly seemed like a prison to me. There was something artificial and dangerous about it.

Many Russian intellectuals fear their children's Americanization, their assimilation into the main-stream "anti-intellectual American culture." As opposed to them, who had come from the society of despotism, where Russian intelligentsia had to assume the passive role of learners and thinkers to escape servitude, their children are living in the free America, a world of mass culture, consumerism, and pragmatic scholarship. They don't read much and they don't read what their parents have read. With horror, we watch them drifting away, not only from our culture, but from our values. Here is the truth that makes this topic especially painful. "They are not *our* children!" But if we impose on them the artificial Russian world, imprinted in our powerful language, would that be the solution to the problem of raising them to be bilingual, intellectual, and inheritors of our idealism? Without any cultural and social context, the media, and the motivation to learn, would that make them "ours?"

Despite my painful longing for my children to be bilingual and bicultural, my heart twisted with pain for the boy locked in his punitive Russian mode. I suddenly wanted him to become an American kid, a healthy monolingual nonintellectual.

For the first year of our new life in New York, our daughter was endlessly sick with colds, infections, flus, and who knows what else. Her pediatrician, an attentive and caring Russian woman, told me, "They all go through this. Culture shock. They cannot cope with their internal struggle, so their body has to resist it. Give her time; she will be okay."

And she was. She acquired English. She became American in her looks and her mannerisms. She does not read much. She does not seem to have any intellectual interests. But she is okay.

Most Russian kids speak English only. My daughter's friends from Leningrad, Kiev, Odessa hardly understand the limited Russian spoken at home and they answer their parents in English. They do not read or write in Russian, not only because they had never learned or forgot, but because they don't want to. They speak English to each other as a confirmation of their American belonging: they are "like everybody else!"

This is similar in some cultural groups but not in others. For example, as far as I know, the situation is quite different in most Chinese families, where, unlike Russian families, children grow up in America fully fluent in Chinese, but the same in Haitian families, where, my adult Haitian students report to me, Haitian children often cannot communicate with their grandmothers who don't speak any English. There must be something in the family structure and family traditions that creates such differences in bilingual development.

Regardless of the social, professional, or intellectual status of any particular family, there is a cultural pattern in families from the same cultural group. This pattern is about power and control in the parent–child relationship, heavily imposed by the ethnic culture. It is possible that in the Chinese family, the tradition of obedience and unquestionable respect to the parents' culture is so strong that the children have no choice but to subjugate themselves to their parents, which makes them keep their language and the surface attributes of the parents' culture. The question is, how many of them would need psychological help?

When I returned from vacation, I got back to my writing. I reread the unfitting pieces for my story about a rosy picture of bilingualism, a celebration of harmony and of successful acculturation where the mother tongue and the mother culture are equally present. I also reread what my daughter had produced about her bilingual experiences and feelings. She did try hard, but only managed to write some strangely awkward unfinished pieces—exactly the same way I had done. I looked at my drafts and at hers. Her writing was mainly about how ugly, how abnormal she feels in Russian; about the horror of the first days in school, when the English spoken classroom felt as an animal roaring; about the crudeness of the kids who did not want to accept her; about how she had to prove herself (to be like everybody else!) to become part of the group. There was nothing positive about speaking or feeling Russian. There was just suffering, and nothing else. My writing and hers had one thing in common: Both of us did not want to talk about it!

The transformation that had occurred in me and made sense of my different selves, nourished and expressed by different languages, led me to the understanding of the multilingual personality as an enriched and harmonic social identity, the whole. If that ever happens to my daughter, it can only happen as a result of her own growth. I am tempted, as all parents do, to substitute my daughter's world and its world-generated values for mine. My writing did not make sense because I wanted my daughter to be me. So, there was no truth and no discovery. The truth is that I want her to be healthy and at peace with herself. I want her to be secure. If I can make her feel comfortable with who she is, Russian or American, she will find strength to grow and, possibly, transform into a truly bilingual, self-asserted, and perhaps intellectual individual. I have to let it go. We can only motivate, but we can't force. Maybe one day she will enjoy being different.

It is crucial to know that our children carry on our ethnic and family culture, language, values, worldviews. That is what makes us feel immortal and helps to deal with the fear of disappearing forever. Transferring culture and language from generation to generation, we ensure life after life and our presence in the future. In his book, *Hunger of Memory* , Richard Rodriguez argued that the price he had to pay for his success in America is the loss of his own culture and language and the emotional distancing from his family. This is the price we, the parents, have to pay for our own and our children's acculturation, for the risk we took by immigrating in pursuit of the American dream. The responsibility of this act is both to the past generations, for cutting off the link with the old culture, and to the generations to come, who will test and value our contributions.

Most of my dear American friends, of Italian, Russian or Eastern European Jewish origins, hardly know anything about their ancestors and their culture. Needless to say, neither their parents nor they speak their language of origin. They belong to this blend, the almost imperceptible chemistry that is called American culture, with a sparkle of something "Russian" or "Italian" in their eyes. There is an avid intellectual interest in their culture of origin and there is a manifest legacy of what is called *national character* in their sense of humor. Very often, there is some transferred cultural pattern of lifestyle: cuisine, hospitality, relationship styles. There are precious memories, even inherited political views, and the attraction to a certain type of people. My American friends' ancestors from Russia speak to me, recognizing my culture as theirs. All of them are liberal intellectuals, former Marxists, and hopeless idealists.

So, I have a chance to be immortal, too. If I can raise my daughter with love and kindness and respect her sense of identity, she might develop the Russian "sparkle." But right now I want her to be healthy and secure. This is the only guarantee that she will integrate in her being free development and at the same time the endurance of the great Russian culture and the powerful Russian language that my father taught her.

The monument on my father's grave represents two hands reaching for each other. One is a big masculine hand, and the other is the hand of a child. The engraving is in two languages: Russian and English.

References

Benesch, S. (1992). Sharing responsibilities: An alternative to the Adjunct Model. *College ESL, 2*(1), 1–10.

Brassens, G. (1963). Les Copains D'Abord. In A Bonnafé (Ed.), *Poésie et Chansons*. Paris: Seghers.

Bruner, J. (1986). *Actual minds, possible worlds*. Cambridge, MA: Harvard University Press.

Hoffman, E. (1989). *Lost in translation*. New York: Penguin.

Igoa, C. (1995). *The inner world of the immigrant child*. New York: St. Martin's Press.

Kingsolver, B. (1991). *Animal dreams*. New York: Harper Perennial.

Krashen, S. (1988). *Second language acquisition and second language learning*. London, New York: Prentice-Hall.

Munaker, S. (1996). *The Great Aha: A Path for Transformation*. Unpublished doctoral dissertation, Union Institute, Cincinnati, OH.

Nabokov, V. (1963). *The gift* (M. Scammell & V. Nabokov, Trans.). New York: Putnam.

Nabokov, V. (1966). *Speak, memory: An autobiography revisited*. New York: Putnam.

Rimbaud, A. (1973). Voýelles. In *Poésiés. Une Saison en Enfer. Illuminations*. Paris: Gallimard.

Triolet, E. (1969). *La Mise en Mots*. Geneva: Skira.

Vian, B. (1968). *Mood Indigo*. (J. Sturrock, Trans.). New York: Grove Press.

Withrow, J., & Price, S. L. (1992). Students investigating language learning. *College ESL, 2*(1), 53–63.